Flight

SIMON & SCHUSTER BOOKS FOR YOUNG READERS
An imprint of Simon & Schuster Children's Publishing Division
1230 Avenue of the Americas, New York, New York 10020

Conceived and produced by Weldon Owen Pty Ltd
59-61 Victoria Street, McMahons Point
Sydney, NSW 2060, Australia

Copyright © 2008 Weldon Owen Pty Ltd
Originally published in the U.K. By Templar Publishing
This edition printed for school book fairs and school book clubs by Simon & Schuster.

WELDON OWEN PTY LTD
Managing Director Kay Scarlett
Publisher Corinne Roberts
Creative Director Sue Burk
Production Director Todd Rechner
Images Manager Trucie Henderson

Concept Development John Bull, The Book Design Company
Project Editor Jasmine Parker
Designer Helen Woodward, Flow Design & Communications
Illustrators Godd.com (Markus Junker, Rolf Schröter, Patrick Tilp), Malcolm Godwin/
Moonrunner Design

Color reproduction by Chroma Graphics (Overseas) Pte Ltd
Printed by Toppan Leefung Printing Ltd
Manufactured in China / 1111 WON

A WELDON OWEN PRODUCTION

SIMON & SCHUSTER BOOKS FOR YOUNG READERS is a trademark of Simon & Schuster, Inc.
The text for this book is set in Meta and Rotis Serif.
10 9 8 7 6 5 4 3 2 1
Library of Congress Control Number: 2010942719
ISBN 978-1-4424-5447-7

Flight

Von Hardesty

Simon & Schuster Books for Young Readers
New York London Toronto Sydney

Contents

...troducing

Understanding Flight

Aviation Ancestors

Aviation Milestones

 **in** *focus*

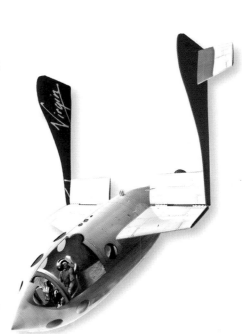

Aircraft

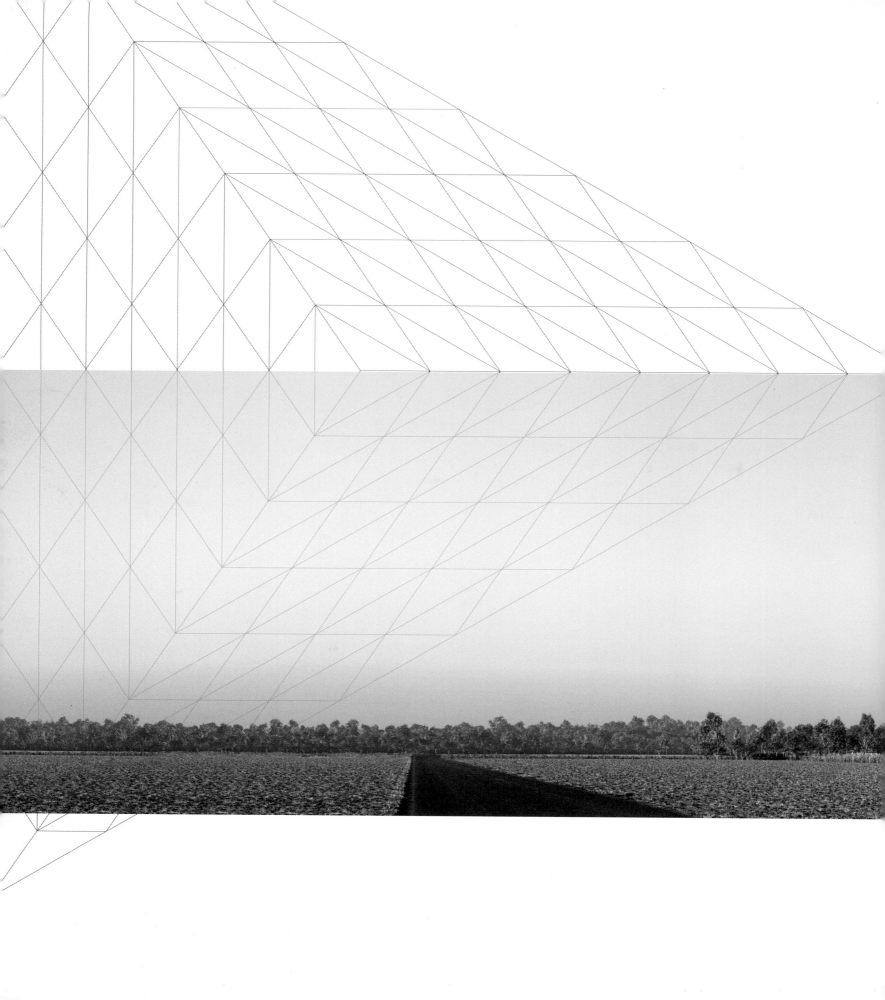

introducing

The Invisible Force

Flight

The story of flight begins with an ancient dream—the human desire to fly like a bird in the sky. Birds are able to overcome gravity by soaring into the air, gliding on rising air, or diving at high speeds. They return to Earth effortlessly. Centuries ago, humans started to copy bird flight. Some made their own wings and attempted to fly by leaping from towers. Leonardo da Vinci designed many wing-flapping aircraft. In 1783, the invention of a hot air balloon allowed people to rise and to float in the air. Humans continued to experiment with soaring machines and gliders to understand wing design and lift. Finally, at the start of the twentieth century, the Wright brothers invented the first powered, controlled flying machine and made flight a reality.

Flying machines

The Learjet 45 and the hot air balloon are two types of flying machine. The balloon is a lighter-than-air vessel, or an aerostat, that flies using a large bag filled with hot air or gas. The Learjet 45 is a heavier-than-air vehicle, or an aerodyne. It has turbofan jet engines that propel it forward, while the flowing shape of the aircraft body, or fuselage, allows it to move easily through the air.

Upward lift *The differences in pressure above and below the wings combine to "lift" the plane in flight.*

Drag behind *The natural resistance of the airplane to move forward through the air is called "drag."*

Forward thrust *The turbofan engines generate enough thrust to propel the plane forward through the air.*

Forces of flight *Four forces act on the Learjet as it flies: gravity (weight), lift (created by the wings), drag (air resistance), and thrust (forward movement by the jet engines).*

Weighed down *Enough lift and thrust have to be created to overcome the weight and downward pull of Earth's gravity on the plane.*

Airfoil wing

The Learjet's wing is an airfoil shape. The airflow passing over the wing's curved upper surface is faster than the airflow passing under the lower surface. This causes a difference in pressure, which lifts or sucks the wing upward.

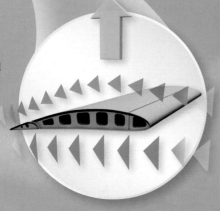

Controlled flight

The wings and tailplanes are equipped with movable control surfaces called elevators, ailerons, and rudders. The pilot uses them to change an airplane's direction and height.

Elevator

Pitch Movement of the nose of the aircraft upward or downward is called "pitch."

Aileron

Roll The wing ailerons control the "roll," or "bank," right or left of the aircraft.

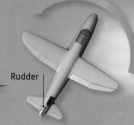

Rudder

Yaw The pilot controls nose left or right, or "yaw," with the rudder on the tail.

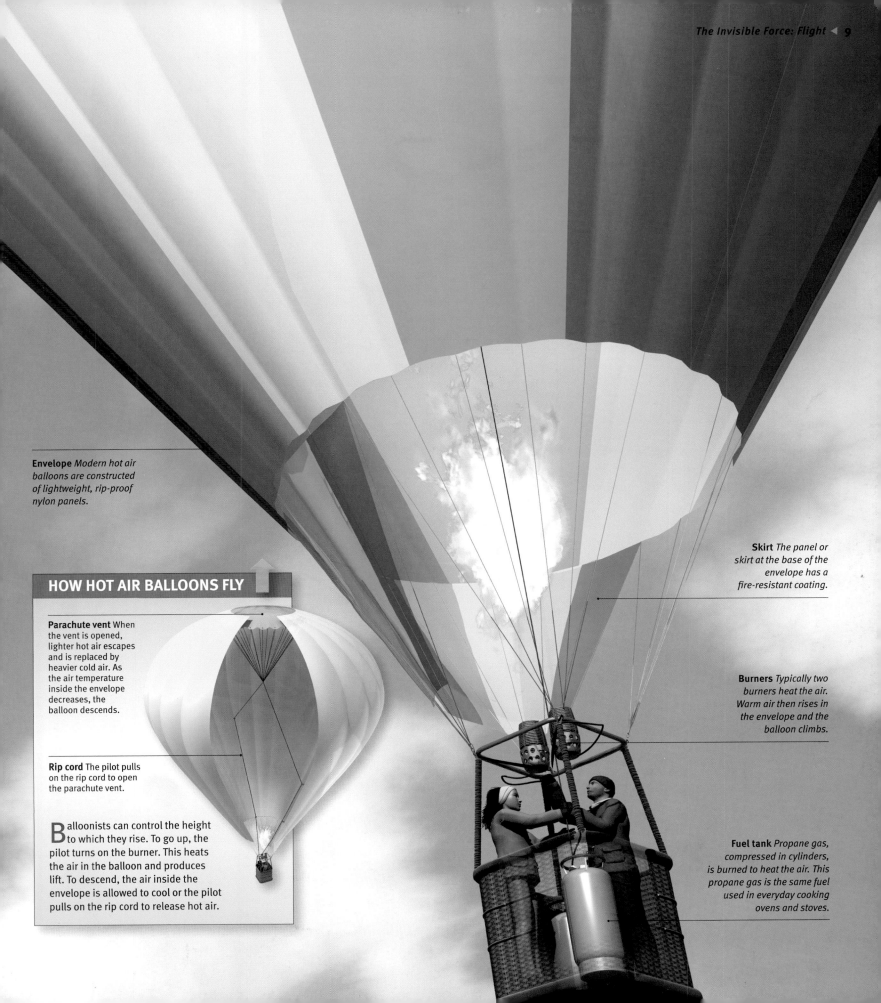

Envelope *Modern hot air balloons are constructed of lightweight, rip-proof nylon panels.*

Skirt *The panel or skirt at the base of the envelope has a fire-resistant coating.*

HOW HOT AIR BALLOONS FLY

Parachute vent When the vent is opened, lighter hot air escapes and is replaced by heavier cold air. As the air temperature inside the envelope decreases, the balloon descends.

Rip cord The pilot pulls on the rip cord to open the parachute vent.

Balloonists can control the height to which they rise. To go up, the pilot turns on the burner. This heats the air in the balloon and produces lift. To descend, the air inside the envelope is allowed to cool or the pilot pulls on the rip cord to release hot air.

Burners *Typically two burners heat the air. Warm air then rises in the envelope and the balloon climbs.*

Fuel tank *Propane gas, compressed in cylinders, is burned to heat the air. This propane gas is the same fuel used in everyday cooking ovens and stoves.*

Observing Nature
Animal Flight

Birds exist everywhere on Earth. They are the only living animals with feathers and come in a huge variety of shapes and sizes. Few other animals can match their flying skills, agility, or speed. Birds can hover in the air, bank sideways, and soar or dive at tremendous speeds. Peregrine falcons can reach 200 miles per hour (320 km/h) when they dive. Flipperlike wings allow some birds to move through water. Some birds rarely fly, and a few species, such as penguins, are incapable of flight. But birds are not the only flying or gliding creatures. Insects also fly or hover by flapping their wings. A bat's wing membrane, supported by its outstretched limbs, enables it to fly long distances. Other animals that take to the air include frogs, lizards, snakes, squirrels, and lemurs.

Primary flight feathers
These wing feathers convert muscle power into thrust, creating forward movement.

Swift and skillful

Swallows maneuver skillfully in pursuit of prey, such as dragonflies and other insects. They are relatively small birds with long, pointed wings, a forked tail, and a streamlined body. As swallows hunt, they perform a series of rapid turns, banks, and swooping movements. They are found on all continents except Antarctica. Their migratory habits are truly impressive; one species journeys seasonally from Britain to southern Africa.

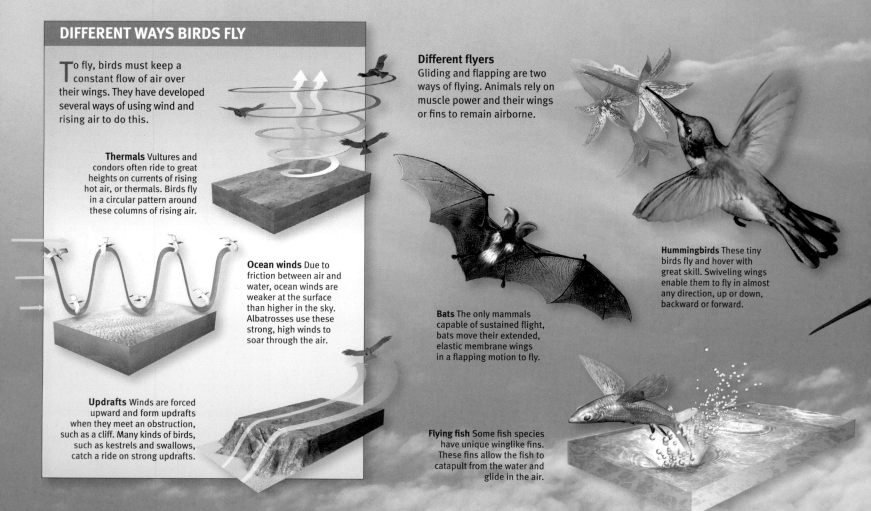

DIFFERENT WAYS BIRDS FLY

To fly, birds must keep a constant flow of air over their wings. They have developed several ways of using wind and rising air to do this.

Thermals Vultures and condors often ride to great heights on currents of rising hot air, or thermals. Birds fly in a circular pattern around these columns of rising air.

Ocean winds Due to friction between air and water, ocean winds are weaker at the surface than higher in the sky. Albatrosses use these strong, high winds to soar through the air.

Updrafts Winds are forced upward and form updrafts when they meet an obstruction, such as a cliff. Many kinds of birds, such as kestrels and swallows, catch a ride on strong updrafts.

Different flyers
Gliding and flapping are two ways of flying. Animals rely on muscle power and their wings or fins to remain airborne.

Bats The only mammals capable of sustained flight, bats move their extended, elastic membrane wings in a flapping motion to fly.

Hummingbirds These tiny birds fly and hover with great skill. Swiveling wings enable them to fly in almost any direction, up or down, backward or forward.

Flying fish Some fish species have unique winglike fins. These fins allow the fish to catapult from the water and glide in the air.

Lightweight bones *The honeycomb structure and internal air sacs inside a bird's wing bones makes them significantly lighter than mammal bones.*

Support system *Reinforced, hollow wing bones make a bird's skeleton sturdy and light enough for flying.*

Doubled up *Like most flying insects, dragonflies have two sets of wings. Their long, flapping wings are very effective for hovering flight.*

Flight engine *Two sets of muscles attached to the breastbone drive the wings up and down. They provide the power that makes it possible for a bird to fly.*

Flight control *Long, forked tail feathers help a swallow regulate its speed, steer, and brake.*

Myths and Legends

Icarus

For many ancient peoples, flight was a mystery. They considered it the domain of the gods or of other magical creatures. Eros, the Greek god of love, and Cupid, his equivalent in Roman mythology, were depicted with wings. Mercury, the Roman god of commerce, was shown with winged cap and sandals. In the Greek legend of Daedalus and Icarus a father and son both flew with wings made from feathers and wax. Winged deities are also prominent in the myths and legends of other cultures. A legend from ancient China tells of the emperor Shun, who flew across his dominions with two reed hats that served as parachutes. Comic-book heroes, such as Superman and Captain Marvel, are modern examples of fantasies connected with flight.

Garuda
In Thai mythology, Garuda, the king of birds, often appeared as an eagle. He battled and slew his sworn enemy, the many-headed serpent, Naga.

ANCIENT MYTHICAL CHARACTERS

Many ancient myths tell of winged gods, angels, and demons. Others recount stories of flying horses and dragons, and even of humans who heroically took to the skies.

Flying king The legendary King Kai Kawus of Persia was carried aloft on his golden throne by four eagles. He kept the eagles flying forward by dangling meat from a pole in front of them.

Winged horse Bellerophon the Valiant, son of the king of Corinth, captured Pegasus, a winged horse. Flying on Pegasus, he slew Chimera, a triple-headed monster.

Queen of spring The Egyptian goddess Queen Isis had wings like a falcon. Each year she flew around Earth and brought spring to the land.

Melting wax wings

Daedalus moved with his son Icarus to the island of Crete. Here he worked for King Minos in the design of the Labyrinth, a huge maze of passages. At the center of this maze lived the Minotaur, a ferocious creature that was half bull and half man. Fearing that King Minos would keep him imprisoned, Daedalus made wings of feathers held together with wax and attached them to his and Icarus's bodies. The pair flew away, but Icarus, excited to find himself aloft, flew too close to the Sun. Its heat melted the wax and he plunged to his death.

Dreams of Flight
Ornithopter

People dreamed of flying for thousands of years before it finally became a reality. Toward the end of the fifteenth century, Leonardo da Vinci designed a unique flying machine modeled on the motion of birds. Known as the ornithopter, the craft had arched wings that would allow a human to fly by flapping them—just like a bird. His concept proved impractical because humans lack the necessary coordination and muscle power to sustain flight with mechanical wings. Still, da Vinci was a brilliant engineer and inventor, who went on to design several futuristic contraptions—known today as the parachute, hang glider, and helicopter. His ideas for flying craft, sketched in his notebooks, were not studied or tested until centuries after his death.

Ancient kites
Kites helped establish the basic principles of aerodynamics that later led to gliders and airplanes. First made of silk and bamboo, kites became lighter and more elaborate once paper was invented.

Chinese kite The first descriptions of Chinese kites date back more than 2,300 years. The Han army occasionally used human kites to scare the enemy.

Japanese kite Brightly colored Japanese kites can be traced back to Chinese Buddhist missionaries who traveled to Japan between AD 649 and 794. The Japanese term for kite, *Kami Tobi*, means "paper hawk." Legends tell of warriors using man-carrying kites to perform heroic deeds.

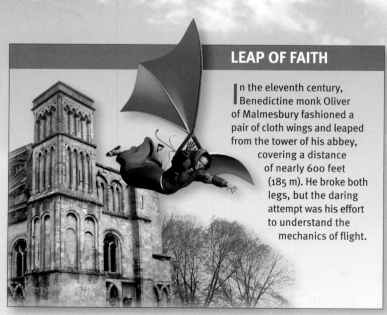

LEAP OF FAITH

In the eleventh century, Benedictine monk Oliver of Malmesbury fashioned a pair of cloth wings and leaped from the tower of his abbey, covering a distance of nearly 600 feet (185 m). He broke both legs, but the daring attempt was his effort to understand the mechanics of flight.

Fusionman
In 2008, Yves Rossy, a Swiss adventurer known as Fusionman, made a remarkable flight in a jet-powered wing. He jumped from a plane, flew for 10 minutes, then landed by parachute.

Backpack machine *The pilot wore a wooden backpack mechanism. A pulley and line system on the harness bent and extended the wings to create a flapping motion.*

Line   Pulley

Backpack

Tension line

Human wings

Leonardo da Vinci carefully studied birds' wings and tried to copy them in his design for the ornithopter. In his idea, the pilot of the ornithopter would take off by leaping from a great height, perhaps a tower or church steeple. He would then move his legs up and down rapidly to raise tension lines attached to his feet. The lines would be linked to a pulley system that controlled the flapping wings.

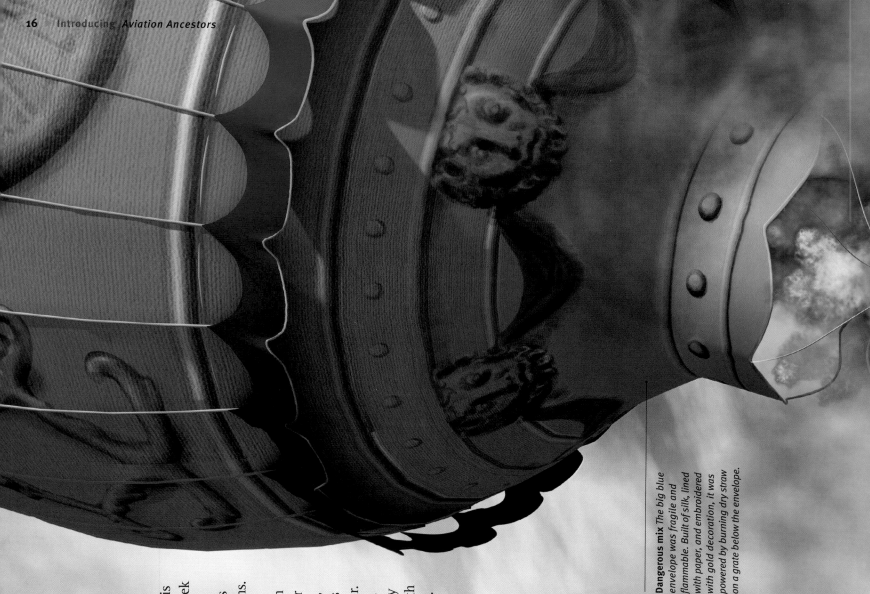

Airships and
Balloons

Hot air rises because it is lighter than cold air. This is the basis for lighter-than-air flight. The ancient Greek mathematician Archimedes was the first to study air buoyancy. In the 1780s, the Montgolfier brothers rediscovered this concept and invented hot air balloons. In 1785, Jean-Pierre François Blanchard and John Jeffries flew over the English Channel in a hydrogen balloon. Balloons became popular and were used for sport flying, atmospheric research, air observation, and exploration. Thaddeus D. C. Lowe used balloons for military air observation in the American Civil War. The first airship, or dirigible, appeared in the 1890s. Count Zeppelin made airships for war and for luxury air travel. In 1926, the airship *Norge* flew to the North Pole. Lighter-than-air flight remains popular today.

Dangerous mix *The big blue envelope was fragile and flammable. Built of silk, lined with paper, and embroidered with gold decoration, it was powered by burning dry straw on a grate below the envelope.*

Breitling Orbiter 3
The Breitling Orbiter 3 made the first around-the-world balloon flight in 1999. From the pressurized gondola, Bertrand Piccard and Brian Jones flew the helium balloon at altitudes of around 30,000 feet (9,145 m).

Ballooning brothers

On September 19, 1783, Joseph and Jacques-Étienne Montgolfier launched their first passenger balloon. At the Palace of Versailles, in France, with King Louis XVI and Queen Marie Antoinette watching, the brothers released a hot air balloon, which rose to an altitude of 1,700 feet (518 m). On board for the eight-minute flight were three animal passengers—a duck, a cockerel, and a sheep. The balloon landed safely. Two months later, two French noblemen made the first balloon flight by humans.

Passengers *The Montgolfier brothers considered a dog, a cow, or a bull for the passenger list on the first hot air balloon flight. In the end, they selected a duck, a cockerel, and a sheep because of their smaller size.*

EARLY BALLOONS AND AIRSHIPS

Balloon design developed rapidly in the nineteenth century. Hydrogen and helium gas balloons proved to be more effective. In time airships appeared; these lighter-than-air vessels had mechanical controls and steering.

Hydrogen balloon As early as 1783, Jacques Alexandre César Charles invented a balloon powered with hydrogen gas. It was 14 times lighter than air and provided good lift for passengers and cargo.

Steam powered In 1852, Henri Giffard flew his airship 17 miles (27 km) from Paris. Its propeller was powered by a small steam engine weighing 250 pounds (112 kg).

Electric battery French aeronauts Charles Renard and Arthur C. Krebs launched the electric-powered airship *La France* in 1884. The long craft had a wooden propeller driven by a battery-powered motor.

Climbing on Rising Air
Gliders

Modern gliders, or sailplanes, have long, slender wings and, like birds, use air currents to soar for hours. Pure gliders do not have an engine or any propulsion system. They move silently through the air, rising and gliding for long distances. Gliders have a long history. Sir George Cayley, the creator of the historic 1853 "coachman carrier," is remembered as the father of modern gliding. In the 1890s, German engineer Otto Lilienthal was the first to demonstrate how gliders could be controlled in flight. The Wright brothers also built a series of gliders to learn the principles of flight. Gliders were used for military purposes in World War II. A glider was built by prisoners of war to escape from imprisonment in Colditz Castle, Germany. When space shuttle orbiters reenter Earth's atmosphere, they land as gliders.

Top tail *The tail assembly was essential for stable flight and control. It became a design feature in modern airplanes.*

Lightweight frame *Cayley used lightweight materials for his glider. He built a wooden frame, which he covered in fabric.*

EARLY GLIDING MODELS

In the nineteenth century, a number of talented experimenters with gliders advanced human understanding of aeronautics: Alphonse Pinaud, Lawrence Hargrave, Hiram Maxim, Percy Sinclair Pilcher, and Otto Lilienthal. In 1891, Lilienthal flew a glider that was the prototype for the modern hang glider.

Cayley glider, 1804
The 1804 glider allowed Cayley to learn more about the principles of flight. The kite-shaped glider featured a fixed wing and an adjustable tail.

Lilienthal glider, 1895
Otto Lilienthal made more than 2,000 flights in gliders. His 1895 glider had curved wings. It also had a form of wing warping, or wing bending, for steering.

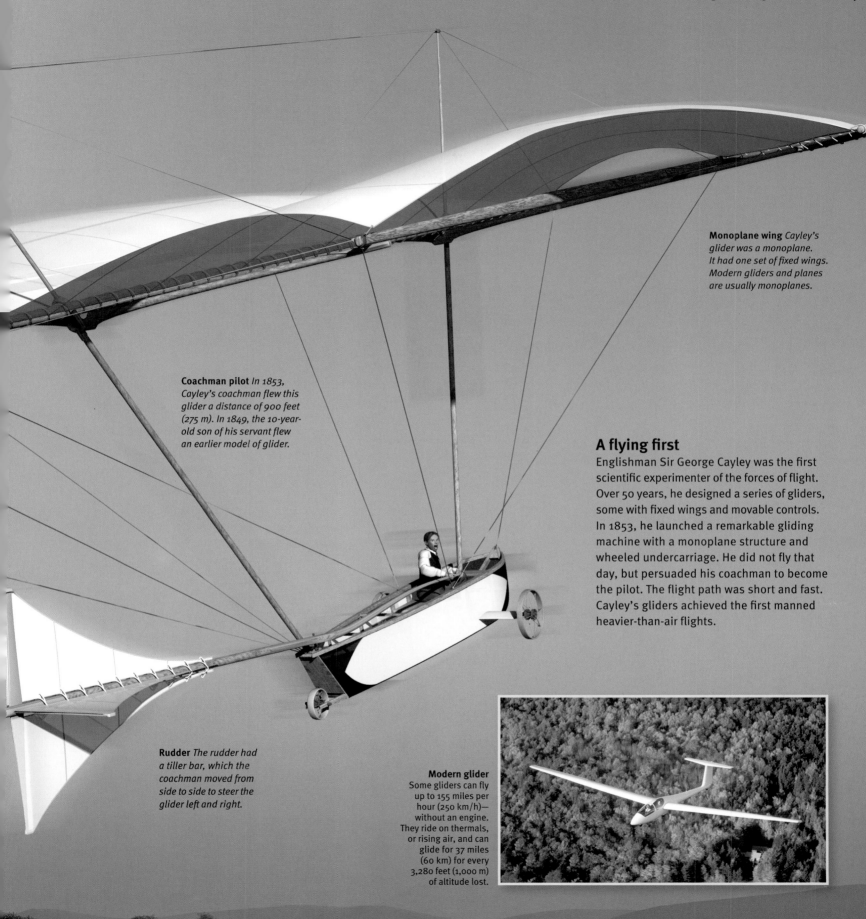

Monoplane wing *Cayley's glider was a monoplane. It had one set of fixed wings. Modern gliders and planes are usually monoplanes.*

Coachman pilot *In 1853, Cayley's coachman flew this glider a distance of 900 feet (275 m). In 1849, the 10-year-old son of his servant flew an earlier model of glider.*

A flying first

Englishman Sir George Cayley was the first scientific experimenter of the forces of flight. Over 50 years, he designed a series of gliders, some with fixed wings and movable controls. In 1853, he launched a remarkable gliding machine with a monoplane structure and wheeled undercarriage. He did not fly that day, but persuaded his coachman to become the pilot. The flight path was short and fast. Cayley's gliders achieved the first manned heavier-than-air flights.

Rudder *The rudder had a tiller bar, which the coachman moved from side to side to steer the glider left and right.*

Modern glider Some gliders can fly up to 155 miles per hour (250 km/h)— without an engine. They ride on thermals, or rising air, and can glide for 37 miles (60 km) for every 3,280 feet (1,000 m) of altitude lost.

Early Flying Machines
Liftoff!

In the late nineteenth century, there was fierce competition among flight pioneers to build a heavier-than-air flying machine. They produced a wide range of contraptions: large and small, and with or without engines. A number of these inventions relied on heavy steam engines to propel them through the air. Most of them had no chance of working. The inventors often worked alone and many had little technical understanding. But by showing what did not work, these failures helped to advance aviation knowledge. It gradually became clear that a successful flying machine would require wings that generated lift, a lightweight engine, and effective flight controls. These were the challenges that confronted aviation inventors at the beginning of the twentieth century.

Red Bull Flugtag event
The Red Bull Flugtag is an event that is held annually in many parts of the world. It is a spirited competition between teams of people who attempt to fly homemade flying machines.

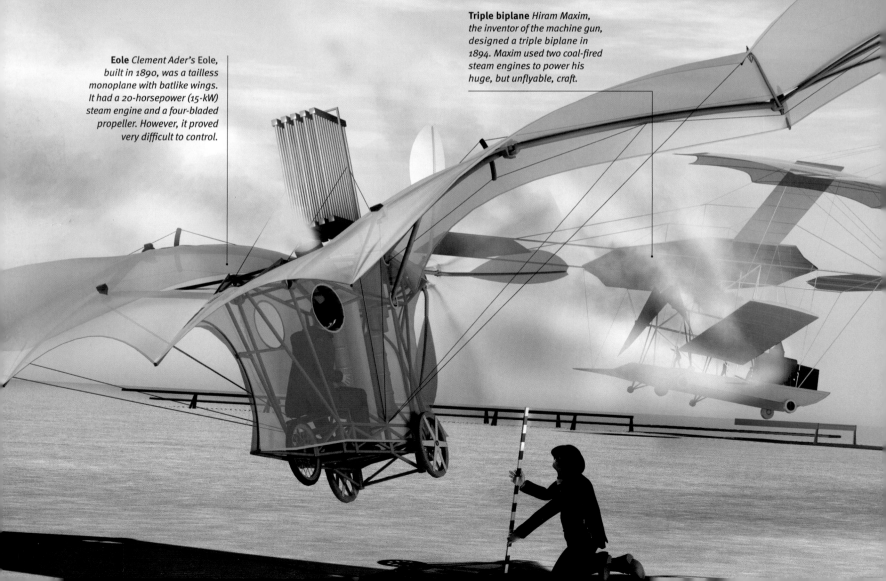

Eole *Clement Ader's Eole, built in 1890, was a tailless monoplane with batlike wings. It had a 20-horsepower (15-kW) steam engine and a four-bladed propeller. However, it proved very difficult to control.*

Triple biplane *Hiram Maxim, the inventor of the machine gun, designed a triple biplane in 1894. Maxim used two coal-fired steam engines to power his huge, but unflyable, craft.*

Strange but interesting

The competition to build a successful airplane produced some interesting, and often strange, results. Clement Ader's *Eole* and Hiram Maxim's triple biplane were failed early efforts at powered flight. They were followed by Trajan Vuia's fanciful "airplane car" monoplane. Santos-Dumont gained popular fame with his huge, tail-first 14-bis. The multiplane of Horatio Phillips featured no fewer than 200 separate wings!

14-bis *In 1906, the Brazilian Santos-Dumont flew his huge and awkward-looking 14-bis. Powered by a 50-horsepower (37-kW) engine, the cloth-covered craft flew 722 feet (220 m) in 21 seconds.*

Airplane car *In 1906–07, Trajan Vuia attached wings and a propeller to his four-wheeled "car." He succeeded numerous times to fly in short hops.*

Multiplane *Horatio Phillips designed his fanciful multiplane in 1907. Even with 200 separate wings, the multiplane managed to get airborne, though only briefly.*

Pistons and Propellers

Early Aircraft

Early aviators flew faster, higher, and farther with each passing year. In 1914, the Russian Igor Sikorsky made a great leap forward with a journey of 800 miles (1,290 km) from St. Petersburg to Kiev. Though plagued with crises, the trip demonstrated the possibility of long-distance flight. The return flight was less dramatic, taking just 14 hours and 38 minutes. Sikorsky's huge flying machine, the *Il'ya Muromets*, named after a legendary Russian warrior, was a four-engine biplane. A crew of three accompanied Sikorsky on this flight. For its time, the *Il'ya Muromets* was a futuristic airplane: It had an enclosed cockpit, a heated cabin with electric lights, a table, and four wicker chairs. There were even onboard meals. Soon after this record-breaking flight, World War I broke out and Sikorsky's remarkable plane was used as a bomber.

Checking the engines *Sikorsky's plane had wooden walkways on the lower wings. These allowed crew members to adjust the engines and provided quick access to an engine that caught fire during the flight to Kiev.*

Cockpit *The enclosed cockpit of the Il'ya Muromets was a radical innovation for the time. The plane had few instruments, but it had a steering wheel instead of a stick.*

Luxury cabin *Like modern airliners, the Il'ya Muromets had a large, well-equipped cabin. It was here that the crew enjoyed their meals on the long trip to Kiev.*

Observation balcony *Sikorsky's aircraft had two observation posts—one a balcony-like extension on the plane's nose, the other a platform with handrails on the upper fuselage.*

HOW A PROPELLER WORKS

As a propeller rotates, air flows around its blades and moves faster over the curved leading edge. This reduces the air pressure in front of the blade and pulls the aircraft forward. Many propellers allow pilots to adjust the blade angle for climbing, cruising, and descending.

Airflow

Piston

Propeller

Argus engines

Early aircraft engines were notoriously unreliable. Sikorsky fitted his *Il'ya Muromets* with lightweight and reliable German Argus engines, which were among the best available. At different times, Sikorsky used German- and British-made engines.

Record-breaking flight

Sikorsky's *Il'ya Muromets* left St. Petersburg for Kiev on June 29, 1914. It made a stop at Orsha for refueling. Over the Dnieper River, a fire broke out in one engine; a crew member walked out on the wing to extinguish it, and the plane landed to make repairs. Later, air turbulence forced the plane into a spin, which Sikorsky skillfully managed to correct. Finally, the *Il'ya Muromets* broke through the clouds above Kiev, passing over the golden domes of the Kiev Pechersk monastery.

Power and Speed
The Jet Age

One of the most important advances in flight history was the invention of the gas turbine jet engine. Jet engines allow the force of heated and flowing gases to turn a turbine and to generate thrust. Experimenters Hans von Ohain and Frank Whittle pioneered this new technology. In 1939, von Ohain's prototype engine powered the first jet airplane—the experimental Heinkel He 178. Independently, Frank Whittle invented a jet engine that was used in British and American jet fighter planes during World War II. Jet-powered fighters and bombers became commonplace, and in the postwar era commercial jet airliners, such as the Boeing 747 jumbo jet, were first used.

Turbo engines

The compressor blades or fans suck air into the combustion chamber, where fuel is continuously burned. This heats and expands the air and produces hot exhaust gases, which drive the turbine and push the aircraft forward. The turbine drives the compressor, and, in the turboshaft engine, an external propeller.

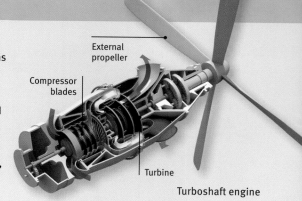

External propeller

Compressor blades

Turbine

Turboshaft engine

First jet fighter

In Germany, Anselm Franz developed an advanced jet engine for the Messerschmitt Me 262—the world's first operational jet fighter.

First turbojet

On August 27, 1939, the Heinkel He 178 lifted off the Marienehe Airfield in Germany. This experimental monoplane was the first aircraft to be powered by the jet thrust from a gas turbine engine. For the pilot, it was a totally new flying experience. The airplane had no propeller. It was powerful, moved easily, and reached speeds greater than 370 miles per hour (595 km/h).

Hot exhaust *Inside the combustion chamber the air mixed with fuel and burned with an explosive force. A jet of hot exhaust gases pushed the aircraft forward.*

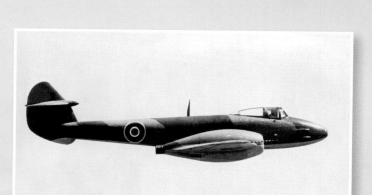

Gloster Meteor

In the 1930s, Frank Whittle worked on his own jet engine design that the British used in their first jet fighter, the Gloster Meteor.

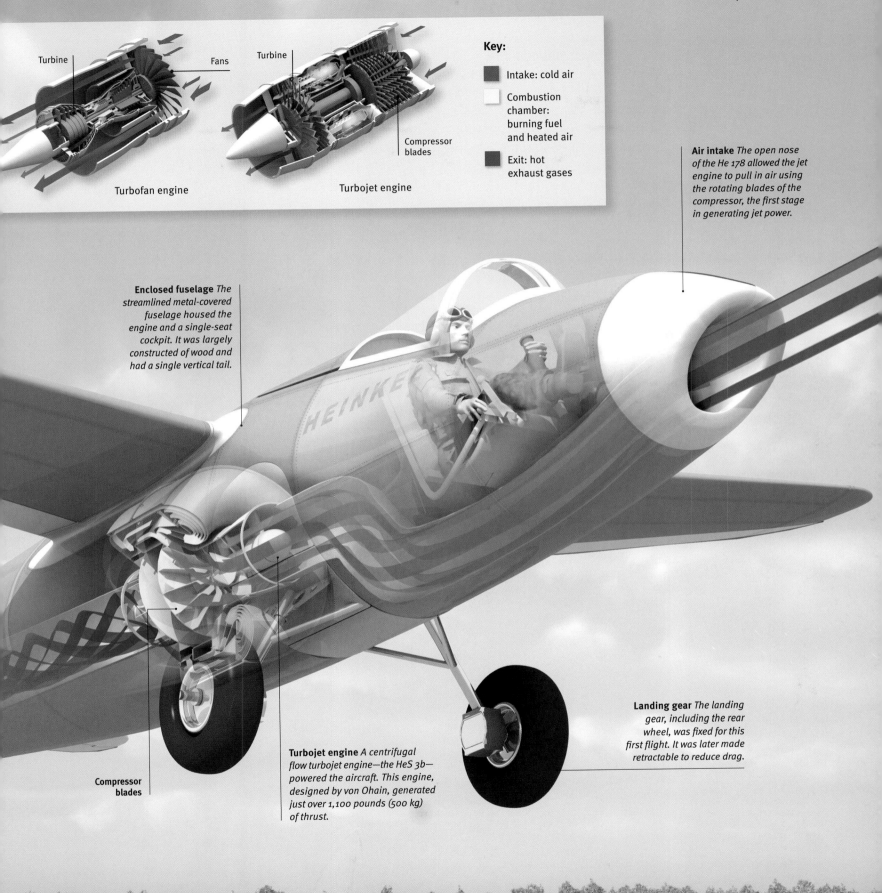

Turbine

Fans

Turbine

Turbofan engine

Compressor blades

Turbojet engine

Key:

■ Intake: cold air

□ Combustion chamber: burning fuel and heated air

■ Exit: hot exhaust gases

Air intake *The open nose of the He 178 allowed the jet engine to pull in air using the rotating blades of the compressor, the first stage in generating jet power.*

Enclosed fuselage *The streamlined metal-covered fuselage housed the engine and a single-seat cockpit. It was largely constructed of wood and had a single vertical tail.*

Compressor blades

Turbojet engine *A centrifugal flow turbojet engine—the HeS 3b—powered the aircraft. This engine, designed by von Ohain, generated just over 1,100 pounds (500 kg) of thrust.*

Landing gear *The landing gear, including the rear wheel, was fixed for this first flight. It was later made retractable to reduce drag.*

Passenger Aircraft

Could the airplane offer humans a fast and safe way to travel across continents and oceans? This possibility arose soon after the Wright brothers made their historic flight in 1903. The slow-moving W8 biplane emerged in 1919. It was one of the first aircraft to carry passengers on short hops between cities. The story of commercial airliners—piston-engine and jet-powered—is filled with breakthroughs. In 1935, the sleek Douglas DC-3 revolutionized air travel. It offered safety, reliability, and comfortable seating for 21 passengers. In the 1950s, the DH106 Comet, the first jet airliner, transformed world air transport. The largest modern airliners are wide-body jets, which carry passengers on most long-haul routes. They include the Boeing 747 and the Airbus A380, which was introduced early in the twenty-first century. Able to carry up to 800 passengers, this giant gives new meaning to the term "jumbo jet." Other kinds of aircraft serve regional, commuter, shuttle, and corporate markets.

Black box

In the tail of every modern airliner is a "black box." Despite its name, it is in fact colored orange. It consists of a flight data recorder (FDR) and a cockpit voice recorder (CVR). These record flight data and communication in the cockpit. The black box can withstand violent impact or extreme heat. Aircraft crash investigations rely on the recovery of these devices.

FLIGHT DATA RECORDER

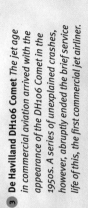

1 **Handley Page W8** *In 1919, the W8 biplane pioneered passenger airline services. It seated up to 15 passengers for short hops between London and continental Europe. In this early airliner, the pilot occupied an open cockpit.*

3 **De Havilland DH106 Comet** *The jet age in commercial aviation arrived with the appearance of the DH106 Comet in the 1950s. A series of unexplained crashes, however, abruptly ended the brief service life of this, the first commercial jet airliner.*

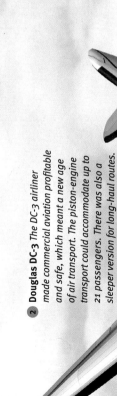

2 **Douglas DC-3** *The DC-3 airliner made commercial aviation profitable and safe, which meant a new age of air transport. The piston-engine transport could accommodate up to 21 passengers. There was also a sleeper version for long-haul routes.*

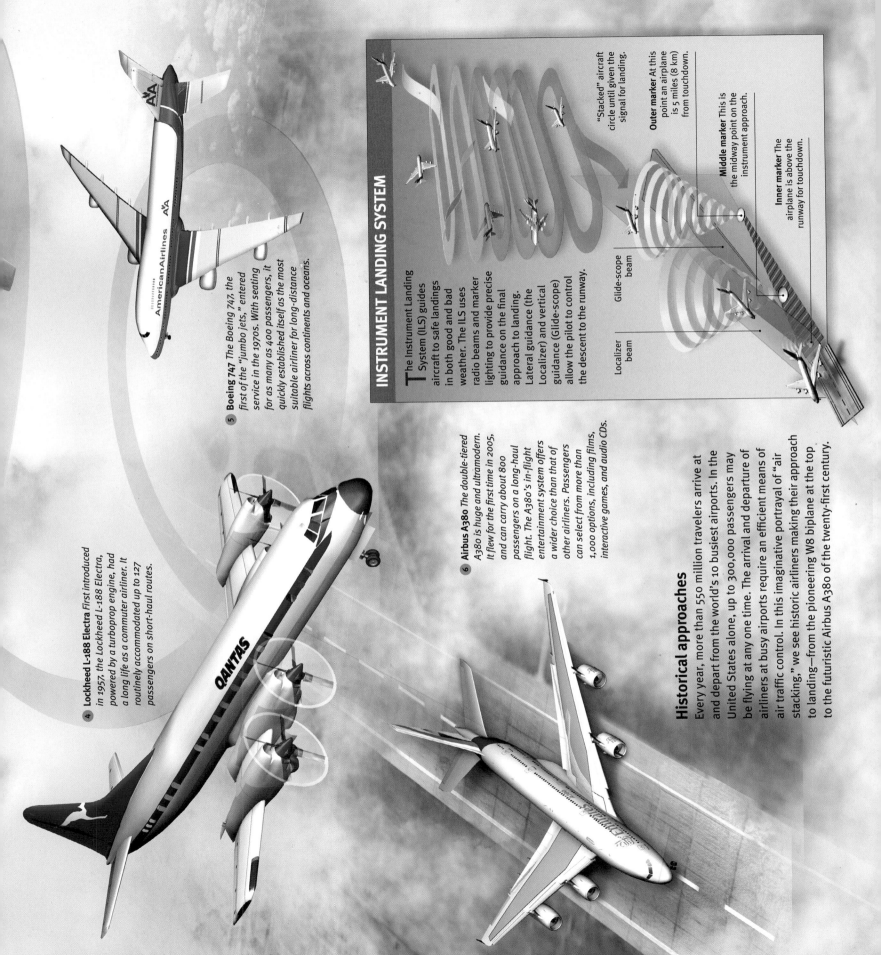

INSTRUMENT LANDING SYSTEM

The Instrument Landing System (ILS) guides aircraft to safe landings in both good and bad weather. The ILS uses radio beams and marker lighting to provide precise guidance on the final approach to landing. Lateral guidance (the Localizer) and vertical guidance (Glide-scope) allow the pilot to control the descent to the runway.

"Stacked" aircraft circle until given the signal for landing.

Outer marker At this point an airplane is 5 miles (8 km) from touchdown.

Middle marker This is the midway point on the instrument approach.

Inner marker The airplane is above the runway for touchdown.

Glide-scope beam

Localizer beam

4 **Lockheed L-188 Electra** *First introduced in 1957, the Lockheed L-188 Electra, powered by a turboprop engine, had a long life as a commuter airliner. It routinely accommodated up to 127 passengers on short-haul routes.*

5 **Boeing 747** *The Boeing 747, the first of the "jumbo jets," entered service in the 1970s. With seating for as many as 400 passengers, it quickly established itself as the most suitable airliner for long-distance flights across continents and oceans.*

6 **Airbus A380** *The double-tiered A380 is huge and ultramodern. It flew for the first time in 2005, and can carry about 800 passengers on a long-haul flight. The A380's in-flight entertainment system offers a wider choice than that of other airliners. Passengers can select from more than 1,000 options, including films, interactive games, and audio CDs.*

Historical approaches

Every year, more than 550 million travelers arrive at and depart from the world's 10 busiest airports. In the United States alone, up to 300,000 passengers may be flying at any one time. The arrival and departure of airliners at busy airports require an efficient means of air traffic control. In this imaginative portrayal of "air stacking," we see historic airliners making their approach to landing—from the pioneering W8 biplane at the top to the futuristic Airbus A380 of the twenty-first century.

Faster Than Sound

Supersonic

During World War II Spitfire and Mustang fighter pilots began to hit a "sonic wall." They struck an invisible barrier when the airplane approached the speed of sound, or Mach 1. They experienced violent shock waves and the plane was hard to control. Breaking the sound barrier became an international challenge. Some test planes shook so violently they broke apart. But on October 14, 1947, Charles "Chuck" Yeager was the first human to fly faster than sound in the Bell X-1. Experiments continued, and in 1953 Scott Crossfield achieved Mach 2 in the Douglas D-558-2 Skyrocket. Flying supersonic became routine for military aviators, while Concorde was the only commercial airliner to offer flights at supersonic speeds until it retired from service in 2003.

Horizontal stabilizer *This could be adjusted upward or downward at high speeds to improve flight control of the aircraft.*

Mothership launch
The short-winged Bell X-1, or *Glamorous Glennis,* named after Chuck Yeager's wife, was launched at an altitude of 23,000 feet (7,000 m) from the bomb bay of a B-29 heavy bomber aircraft.

Rocket-engine plume *The engine generated 6,000 pounds (2,722 kg) of thrust. The short-lived burn lasted only 2.5 minutes.*

CONCORDE 1969–2003

Concorde cruised at 1,320 miles per hour (2,124 km/h), or Mach 2.2. It could fly from Paris to New York in 3.5 hours and had a movable nose to increase visibility and streamlining.

Nose up and streamlined

5 degrees down for landing

12.5 degrees down for taxiing and takeoff

Wings *The short, thin wings could withstand supersonic flight, but not conventional takeoff or landing. The craft glided to a landing.*

Fuselage *The streamlined fuselage of the Bell X-1 was shaped like a supersonic .50 caliber machine-gun bullet.*

Cockpit *The tiny cockpit of the Bell X-1 had limited visibility. There was no ejection seat or emergency exit for the pilot.*

High-speed probe *At the end of the nose was a narrow probe to gather data on air pressure during the flight.*

GLAMOROUS GLENNIS

Breaking the barrier

Shock waves ripped across the desert floor in California when Chuck Yeager broke the sound barrier. The bullet-shaped experimental craft was powered by a four-chamber rocket engine burning liquid oxygen and ethyl alcohol. Approaching transonic speed—the speed of sound—the Bell X-1 encountered turbulence and marginal loss of control. Mach 1.06 was reached at 43,000 feet (13,000 m). The supersonic age had arrived.

The sound barrier

When an airplane flies transonic, it encounters shock waves of compressed air. Some people believed that it was impossible to fly through the sound barrier because of this "compressibility" of air. But the Bell X-1 proved that the barrier could be broken.

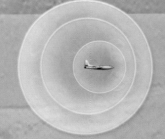

Subsonic Below Mach 1, the pressure waves radiate in front of, as well as behind, the airplane.

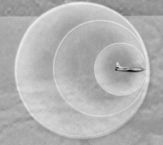

Transonic At Mach 1, the plane catches up with its own pressure waves, which build up into a shock wave.

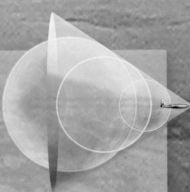

Supersonic Above Mach 1, the shock waves form a cone. This causes a sonic boom when it hits the ground.

Space Flight

The space shuttle made its first orbital flight in 1981, and it was the world's first reusable spacecraft. Over a decade had passed since the Apollo 11 astronauts Neil Armstrong and Buzz Aldrin had walked on the Moon. Unlike those early lunar missions, the purpose of the space shuttle was to complete only near-Earth orbital flights. The shuttle, or "space plane," was key in this new Space Transportation System (STS). The first vehicle had impressive features: 49 engines, 23 antennae, five computers, dual flight controls, electric-power generators, and onboard life-support systems. Since the first voyage, space shuttles have made regular missions into Earth's orbit. They release communications satellites, engage in scientific research, and service orbiting space stations. One of the most memorable missions was the delivery and placement of the Hubble Space Telescope.

***Atlantis* controls**
The *Atlantis* cockpit houses an advanced computer-assisted flight control system called a "glass cockpit." It has electronic instrument displays instead of older mechanical gauges and the pilot uses digital fly-by-wire controls.

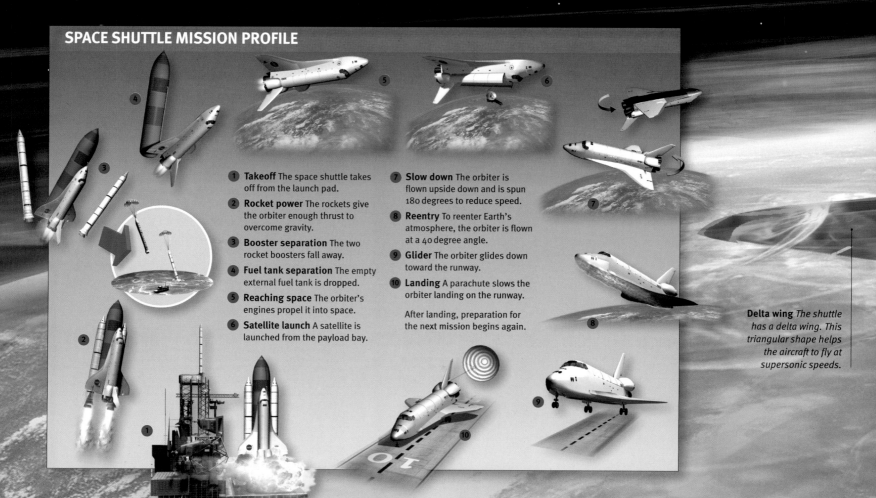

SPACE SHUTTLE MISSION PROFILE

1. **Takeoff** The space shuttle takes off from the launch pad.
2. **Rocket power** The rockets give the orbiter enough thrust to overcome gravity.
3. **Booster separation** The two rocket boosters fall away.
4. **Fuel tank separation** The empty external fuel tank is dropped.
5. **Reaching space** The orbiter's engines propel it into space.
6. **Satellite launch** A satellite is launched from the payload bay.
7. **Slow down** The orbiter is flown upside down and is spun 180 degrees to reduce speed.
8. **Reentry** To reenter Earth's atmosphere, the orbiter is flown at a 40 degree angle.
9. **Glider** The orbiter glides down toward the runway.
10. **Landing** A parachute slows the orbiter landing on the runway.

After landing, preparation for the next mission begins again.

Delta wing *The shuttle has a delta wing. This triangular shape helps the aircraft to fly at supersonic speeds.*

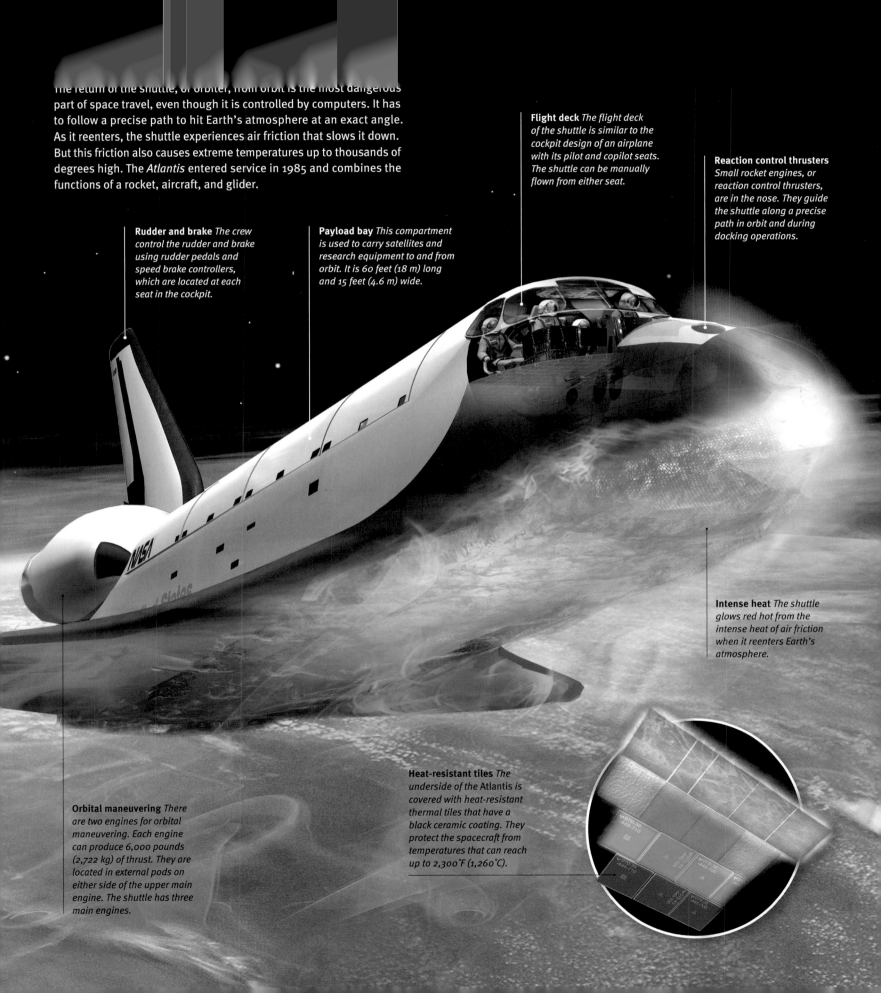

The return of the shuttle, or orbiter, from orbit is the most dangerous part of space travel, even though it is controlled by computers. It has to follow a precise path to hit Earth's atmosphere at an exact angle. As it reenters, the shuttle experiences air friction that slows it down. But this friction also causes extreme temperatures up to thousands of degrees high. The *Atlantis* entered service in 1985 and combines the functions of a rocket, aircraft, and glider.

Flight deck *The flight deck of the shuttle is similar to the cockpit design of an airplane with its pilot and copilot seats. The shuttle can be manually flown from either seat.*

Reaction control thrusters *Small rocket engines, or reaction control thrusters, are in the nose. They guide the shuttle along a precise path in orbit and during docking operations.*

Rudder and brake *The crew control the rudder and brake using rudder pedals and speed brake controllers, which are located at each seat in the cockpit.*

Payload bay *This compartment is used to carry satellites and research equipment to and from orbit. It is 60 feet (18 m) long and 15 feet (4.6 m) wide.*

Intense heat *The shuttle glows red hot from the intense heat of air friction when it reenters Earth's atmosphere.*

Orbital maneuvering *There are two engines for orbital maneuvering. Each engine can produce 6,000 pounds (2,722 kg) of thrust. They are located in external pods on either side of the upper main engine. The shuttle has three main engines.*

Heat-resistant tiles *The underside of the* Atlantis *is covered with heat-resistant thermal tiles that have a black ceramic coating. They protect the spacecraft from temperatures that can reach up to 2,300°F (1,260°C).*

Photo feature This photo shows the aircraft featured on each spread.

BLÉRIOT XI: THE FACTS

LENGTH: 26 feet (8 m)

WINGSPAN: 25.6 feet (7.8 m)

WEIGHT: 220.5 pounds (100 kg)

ENGINE: Three-cylinder Italian Anzani

CREW AND PASSENGERS: One pilot

Fast facts Fast facts at your fingertips give you essential information about each aircraft.

Speed gauge This gauge shows the top speed of the aircraft.

TOP SPEED

2,170 mph (3,500 km/h)

1,860 mph (3,000 km/h)

1,550 mph (2,500 km/h)

1,240 mph (2,000 km/h)

930 mph (1,500 km/h)

Mach 1

620 mph (1,000 km/h)

310 mph (500 km/h)

Flyer 28 mph (45 km/h)

0

WRIGHT FLYER: THE FACTS

LENGTH: 21 feet (6.4 m)

WINGSPAN: 40.4 feet (12.3 m)

WEIGHT: 817.9 pounds (371 kg)

ENGINE: Horizontal, four-cylinder, water-cooled

CREW AND PASSENGERS: One pilot

Wright Flyer

On December 17, 1903, Orville and Wilbur Wright made history and launched the age of aviation. Their Flyer achieved the world's first controlled and powered heavier-than-air flight. It was a short, low flight over the windswept sands of Kitty Hawk, North Carolina. The biggest difficulties were keeping the nose level and maintaining control to avoid crashing. The Wright brothers continued to improve this design and their 1905 Flyer became the world's first practical airplane. It could fly for up to half an hour and complete figure-of-eight turns around pylons. The Wright brothers learned how to fly by watching birds. They also built their own wind tunnel to test air flow over model wings and experimented with gliders. Their engineering skills and imagination ultimately led to their aviation success.

Launch trolley *The Wrights built a 60-foot (18-m) launch rail that looked like a railroad track. On takeoff, the Flyer rode down the track on a small wheeled dolly.*

The Wright brothers
Wilbur Wright (1867–1912) and Orville Wright (1871–1948) from Dayton, Ohio, were bicycle mechanics. At school they dreamed of flying and sold kites to their classmates. When they were young men, they opened a bicycle business and used the profits to build aircraft.

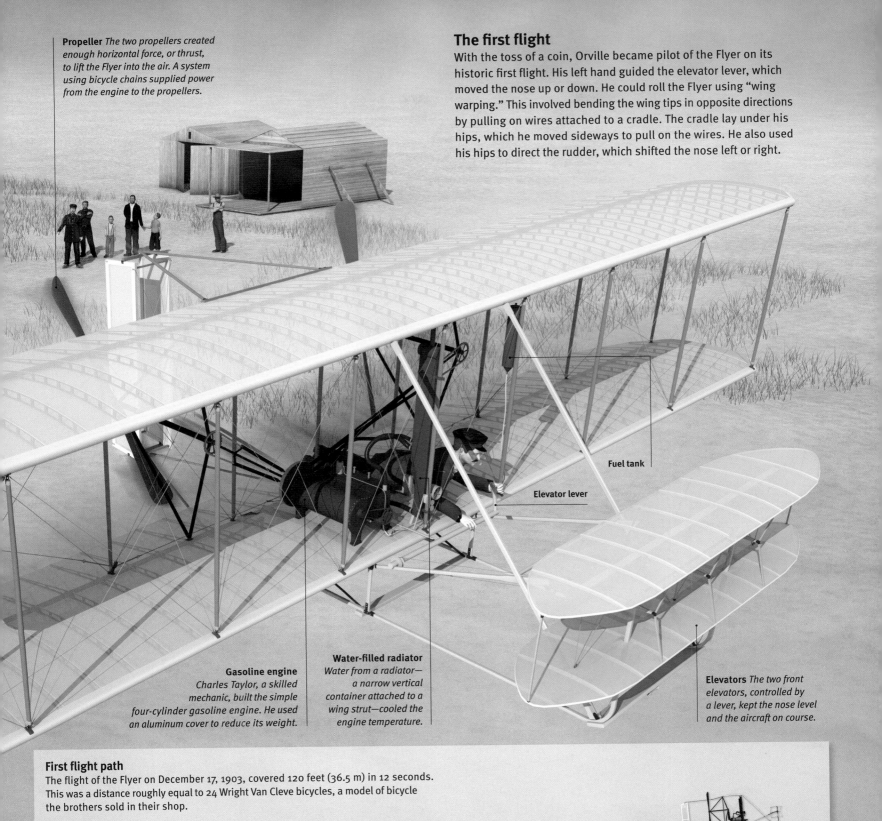

Propeller *The two propellers created enough horizontal force, or thrust, to lift the Flyer into the air. A system using bicycle chains supplied power from the engine to the propellers.*

The first flight

With the toss of a coin, Orville became pilot of the Flyer on its historic first flight. His left hand guided the elevator lever, which moved the nose up or down. He could roll the Flyer using "wing warping." This involved bending the wing tips in opposite directions by pulling on wires attached to a cradle. The cradle lay under his hips, which he moved sideways to pull on the wires. He also used his hips to direct the rudder, which shifted the nose left or right.

Fuel tank

Elevator lever

Gasoline engine *Charles Taylor, a skilled mechanic, built the simple four-cylinder gasoline engine. He used an aluminum cover to reduce its weight.*

Water-filled radiator *Water from a radiator— a narrow vertical container attached to a wing strut—cooled the engine temperature.*

Elevators *The two front elevators, controlled by a lever, kept the nose level and the aircraft on course.*

First flight path

The flight of the Flyer on December 17, 1903, covered 120 feet (36.5 m) in 12 seconds. This was a distance roughly equal to 24 Wright Van Cleve bicycles, a model of bicycle the brothers sold in their shop.

BLÉRIOT XI: THE FACTS

LENGTH:	26 feet (8 m)
WINGSPAN:	25.6 feet (7.8 m)
WEIGHT:	220.5 pounds (100 kg)
ENGINE:	Three-cylinder Italian Anzani
CREW AND PASSENGERS:	One pilot

Wing covering *The wing sections were covered with fabric. The fuselage was partially covered in fabric and reinforced with steel tubing.*

Crossing the Channel
Blériot XI

At the beginning of the twentieth century, pilots competed fiercely to fly faster, higher, and further. In 1909, Britain's *Daily Mail* newspaper offered a prize of £1,000 (US$1,820) for the first aviator to cross the English Channel from either side. Frenchman Louis Blériot, an engineer and fearless pilot, took up the challenge and, against all odds, successfully flew across the English Channel from near Calais, France, to Dover, England. Overnight, Blériot became a celebrity. The small Blériot XI monoplane had broken the isolation of England from the European continent.

Rudder

Channel flight path
Blériot flew a flight path from the sand dunes of the French coast at Sangatte beach near Calais to the White Cliffs of Dover.

ENGLAND

London

Dover
Calais

Sangatte

Paris

FRANCE

TOP SPEED 0 | Blériot XI 47 mph (75 km/h) | 620 mph (1,000 km/h) | Mach 1 | 930 mph (1,500 km/h) | 1,240 mph (2,000 km/h) | 1,550 mph (2,500 km/h) | 1,860 mph (3,000 km/h) | 2,170 mph (3,500 km/h)

Channel crossing

Frenchman Louis Blériot took off from Sangatte beach, near Calais, France, at dawn on the morning of July 25, 1909. He aimed to be the first man to fly across the English Channel. Dressed in overalls and a leather helmet, he steered his fragile wood and fabric airplane over the Channel waters and through mist. He did not have a compass or a map. His plane cruised at 40 miles per hour (64 km/h). The flight lasted 37 minutes and finished with a hard landing on the White Cliffs of Dover.

Propeller *Blériot fitted his aircraft with a two-bladed wooden propeller. On the day of the flight, a dog strayed into the propeller and was killed.*

Fuel capsule

Landing gear *One of the most innovative features of the Blériot XI was the landing gear. Blériot used rubber bands to make shock absorbers on the wheels.*

Wing structure *The wing was made of ash wood and fabric, which reduced weight and drag. "Wing warping," or bending, was used to control the airplane's roll movements.*

CRASH LANDING

Blériot battled wind gusts and a severely overheating engine to make a rushed downhill landing near Dover Castle that shattered his propeller and landing gear.

Blériot with his wife and plane after the crash

2,170 mph
(3,500 km/h)

1,860 mph
(3,000 km/h)

1,550 mph
(2,500 km/h)

1,240 mph
(2,000 km/h)

930 mph
(1,500 km/h)

Mach 1

620 mph
(1,000 km/h)

SPAD XIII 135 mph
(218 km/h)

0

TOP SPEED

SPAD XIII: THE FACTS

LENGTH:	20.7 feet (6.3 m)
WINGSPAN:	26.9 feet (8.2 m)
WEIGHT:	1,254 pounds (569 kg)
ENGINE:	Hispano Suiza 8 Be
CREW AND PASSENGERS:	One pilot

Aerial Combat

SPAD XIII

A sudden and fiery death threatened all pilots during World War I (1914–1918). The first "dogfight"—aerial combat between aircraft—was in April 1915, when French pilot Roland Garros shot down a German airplane. Both sides then scrambled to arm their aircraft and develop new aerial tactics. Military aircraft advanced rapidly as a weapon of war, with improved designs, more powerful engines, and devastating armament. Soon "lone wolf" operations were replaced with squadron-size formations in the quest to gain dominance in the air. When a pilot shot down five or more aircraft, he joined the legendary ranks of the "aces," which include Manfred von Richthofen, Georges Guynemer, William Bishop, and Eddie Rickenbacker. World War I shaped the future of military aviation.

Deadly dogfight

Aerial dogfights drew battling aircraft into close quarters. When attacking an enemy, a pilot often dived from the Sun or used clouds for cover. Air combat was sudden, intense, short-lived, and could be deadly. This World War I scene shows an American SPAD XIII pursued by a German Fokker D.VII. The Fokker D.VIIs are making a counterattack to defend their Junkers Cl.I J10 bomber, which is retreating from the arena of combat.

Defensive attack *Another German Fokker D.VII approaches swiftly to join the air battle and provide cover for the attacking Fokker. Ernst Udet, flying No. 14, was the second-highest scoring German ace.*

French SPAD XIII The French air force painted hues and camouflage patterns.

British scheme basic The British Royal Flying Corps had standard camouflage.

German lavender lozenge German planes used lavender colors for camouflage.

Creative camouflage

As World War I progressed, both Allied and German forces used paint and special markings on warplanes to make them harder for enemies to detect. Many camouflage patterns were elaborate and colorful.

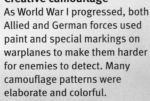

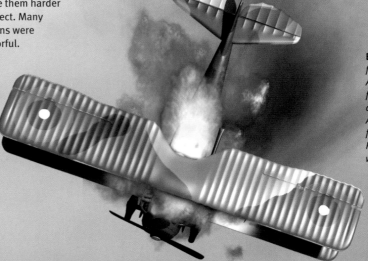

Ball of flames *A SPAD XIII falls from the sky in flames. Aircraft were vulnerable to fire and disintegration once attacked by machine guns. Attacking fighters aimed for the engine or fuel tanks. Pilots and observers flew without parachutes.*

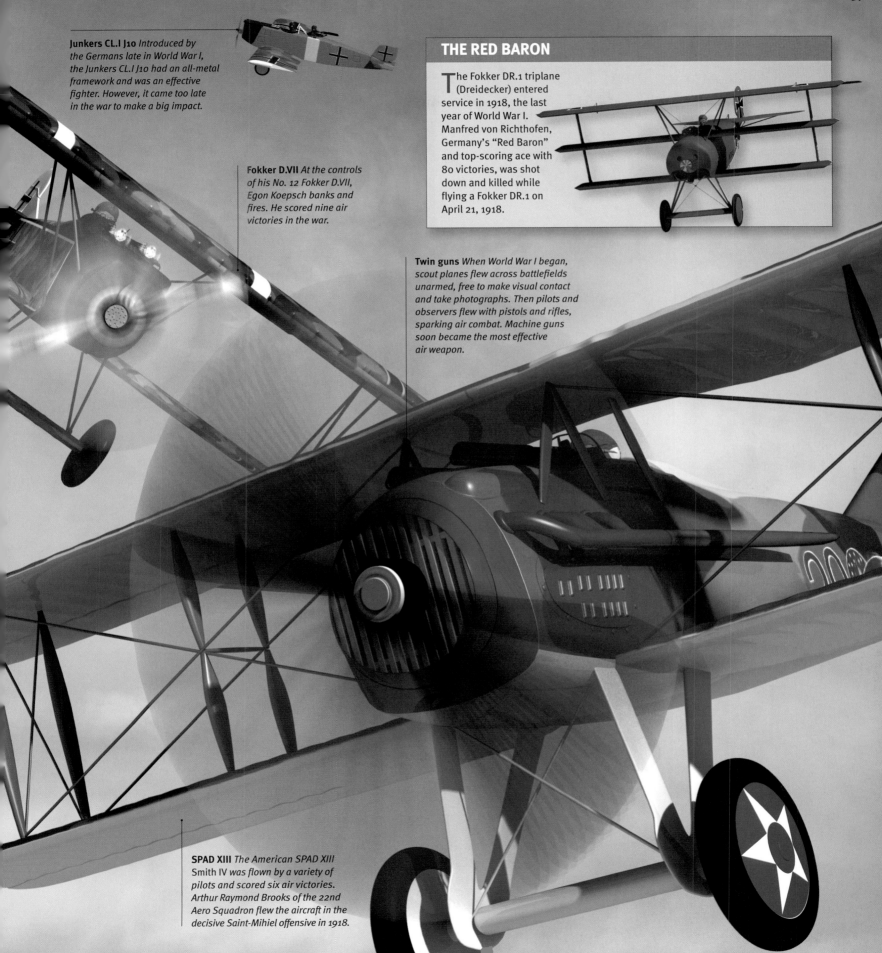

Junkers CL.I J10 *Introduced by the Germans late in World War I, the Junkers CL.I J10 had an all-metal framework and was an effective fighter. However, it came too late in the war to make a big impact.*

THE RED BARON

T he Fokker DR.1 triplane (Dreidecker) entered service in 1918, the last year of World War I. Manfred von Richthofen, Germany's "Red Baron" and top-scoring ace with 80 victories, was shot down and killed while flying a Fokker DR.1 on April 21, 1918.

Fokker D.VII *At the controls of his No. 12 Fokker D.VII, Egon Koepsch banks and fires. He scored nine air victories in the war.*

Twin guns *When World War I began, scout planes flew across battlefields unarmed, free to make visual contact and take photographs. Then pilots and observers flew with pistols and rifles, sparking air combat. Machine guns soon became the most effective air weapon.*

SPAD XIII *The American SPAD XIII Smith IV was flown by a variety of pilots and scored six air victories. Arthur Raymond Brooks of the 22nd Aero Squadron flew the aircraft in the decisive Saint-Mihiel offensive in 1918.*

TOP SPEED 0 · Racer 317 mph (472 km/h) · 620 mph (1,000 km/h) · Mach 1 · 930 mph (1,500 km/h) · 1,240 mph (2,000 km/h) · 1,550 mph (2,500 km/h) · 1,860 mph (3,000 km/h) · 2,170 mph (3,500 km/h)

WEDDELL-WILLIAMS: THE FACTS

LENGTH: 23.3 feet (7.1 m)

WINGSPAN: 26.6 feet (8.1 m)

WEIGHT: 1,510 pounds (685 kg)

ENGINE: Pratt & Whitney Wasp Junior

CREW AND PASSENGERS: One pilot

Weddell-Williams

Racer

Air racing became popular in the 1920s with competition for the Schneider Cup for seaplanes and the Pulitzer Trophy for land planes. Some of the most famous pilots of the time competed in these air races. In the 1930s, pilots Jim Weddell and Harry Williams designed some of the fastest racing planes. Their Weddell-Williams aircraft competed successfully in the National Air Races held at Cleveland, Ohio, in the United States. A cross-country race from California to Cleveland kicked off this annual event. But to win the celebrated Thompson Trophy, pilots raced around a tough 10-mile (16-km) closed circuit for either 100 miles (160 km) or 300 miles (480 km). Crowds looked on as daredevil pilots sped down straight runs and around pylons.

Gee Bee *Jimmy Doolittle won the Thompson Trophy in 1932, flying a Gee Bee at the record speed of 252.7 miles per hour (406.7 km/h).*

Weddell-Williams No. 44
In 1933, Jim Weddell flew his No. 44 racer to win the Thompson Trophy at a speed of 237.9 miles per hour (382.9 km/h).

TYPES OF STUNTS

Thrilling aerobatics by pilots, using great skill and agility, have been part of air shows since around the end of World War I. Russian pilot Peter Nesterov performed the first loop in 1912.

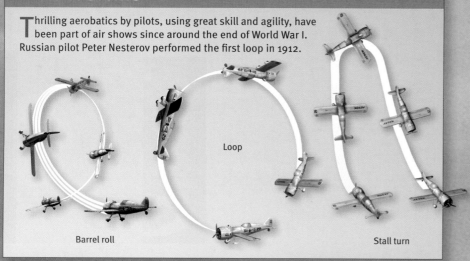

Loop

Barrel roll

Stall turn

Racing forward

The 1930s racing planes relied on powerful engines for their speed rather than streamlining. This often made them dangerous. The Gee Bee was fast, but the combination of short wings and a powerful engine made it hard to control. Every Gee Bee that was built crashed, killing five racing pilots and even the designer. But these races were important for the development of flight. They encouraged all aviators to challenge speed and distance records.

National Air Races
The National Air Races were held every year from 1920 until 1949. Crowds watched aerobatics, airships, gliders, parachute jumping and a "Women's Air Derby."

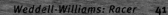

Amelia Earhart Twenty-three female pilots, including Amelia Earhart, entered the first women's air race. In the 1930s, she set records for speed and altitude for female pilots. She disappeared in 1937 attempting a new around-the-world record.

Weddell-Williams No. 92
In 1932, pilot Jimmy Haizlip won the Bendix Trophy in the Weddell-Williams No. 92.

2,170 mph (3,500 km/h)

1,860 mph (3,000 km/h)

1,550 mph (2,500 km/h)

1,240 mph (2,000 km/h)

930 mph (1,500 km/h)

Mach 1

620 mph (1,000 km/h)

Lancaster 272 mph (438 km/h)

TOP SPEED 0

AVRO LANCASTER: THE FACTS

LENGTH:	69.6 feet (21.2 m)
WINGSPAN:	102 feet (31.1 m)
WEIGHT:	36,828 pounds (16,705 kg)
ENGINE:	Four Rolls Royce Merlin engines
CREW AND PASSENGERS:	One pilot; six crew

Avro
Lancaster

The Avro Lancaster bomber played a major role in the Allied strategic bombing campaign against Nazi Germany in World War II. Standing 19 feet (5.8 m) tall on the tarmac, the Lancaster was the UK Royal Air Force's (RAF) most effective night bomber. Lancaster crews flew more than 150,000 flight operations, or "sorties," against the enemy. The first generation of powerful Lancaster bombers, the MK-1 series, was introduced in 1941. The four-engine bomber had eight machine guns and a bomb bay that could carry a payload of up to 22,000 pounds (10,000 kg). The RAF bombers brought destruction to urban and industrial targets in Germany. In the most famous "Grand Slam" mission of 1945, a squadron of Lancasters known as the "Dam Busters" destroyed the Bielefeld Viaduct.

Night operation

While traveling to a target, a Lancaster bomber faced fierce enemy antiaircraft fire and night fighters. Night operations were highly dangerous. Exploding shells, or "flak," could hit a bomber suddenly without warning. The RAF bombers were painted dark green and brown to camouflage them from enemy detection. But the night fighters of the German Luftwaffe used radar to detect and shoot the bombers down.

Radio operator

Forward machine gun
The bombardier operated the forward machine gun if an enemy fighter came into range.

Bombardier *In the nose, the bombardier, or artilleryman, stretched out behind the forward plastic cover. He pinpointed the target before releasing the bombs.*

Cramped conditions *Night missions were cramped inside the Lancaster bomber. Flying at high altitude, the crew required special flight gear and oxygen.*

Seven-man crew *The crew consisted of a pilot, a copilot who was a flight engineer, a bombardier, a navigator, a radio operator, and two rear gunners.*

Navigator *The navigator sat behind a curtain, so that the light he used to read maps could not be seen by the enemy.*

Down in flames *It is estimated that the RAF lost about 3,920 Lancaster bombers in World War II. Often a direct hit resulted in loss of the bomber and all the crew.*

Enola Gay

The Boeing B-29 Superfortress *Enola Gay* is the most famous strategic bomber of World War II. On August 6, 1945, the *Enola Gay* dropped the first atomic bomb on the city of Hiroshima, Japan.

Top turret *From this key defensive position, a gunner operated two machine guns. Temperatures could be –40°F (–40°C), so crew in the rear had to wear extra clothing to survive the cold.*

Tail gunner *Enemy fighters often attacked Lancaster bombers from behind and below. The tail gun position was heavily armed with four Browning .303 machine guns.*

Speed scale (left margin):
- 2,170 mph (3,500 km/h)
- 1,860 mph (3,000 km/h)
- 1,550 mph (2,500 km/h)
- 1,240 mph (2,000 km/h)
- 930 mph (1,500 km/h)
- Mach 1
- 620 mph (1,000 km/h)
- Guba II 196 mph (314 km/h)
- TOP SPEED 0

CATALINA *GUBA II*: THE FACTS

LENGTH:	64 feet (19.5 m)
WINGSPAN:	104 feet (31.7 m)
WEIGHT:	2,002 pounds (908 kg)
ENGINE:	Two 825-hp (625-kW) Pratt & Whitney Wasp radial engines
CREW AND PASSENGERS:	Two crew; 10 passengers

ACCESS ALL AREAS

The Dornier Do 228 is capable of landing in a short distance by using standard landing gear or skis. This turboprop aircraft is ideal for rescue and firefighting missions and emergency medical airlift flights.

Catalina *Guba II*
Seaplane

In 1938, the American Museum of Natural History sponsored Richard Archbold to explore the Pacific island of New Guinea. The expedition required a seaplane to investigate rivers and lakes in the highlands of the remote, mostly unexplored island. Archbold chose a Consolidated PBY Catalina, which he dubbed the *Guba II*. The all-metal flying boat had a wide, shallow hull and enough room for two crew members, 10 passengers, and cargo consisting of research equipment, tents, and provisions. Archbold and his scientific team eventually piloted the flying boat over the mountainous interior of New Guinea and made a dramatic landing on a large lake. Here they discovered an isolated community of small villages and cultivated fields.

Hidden world

Richard Archbold's Catalina *Guba II* landed on remote Lake Habbema, surrounded by towering mountain peaks, in the highlands of New Guinea. The expedition discovered a previously unknown population of around 60,000 people. The isolated community lived in small rectangular structures, maintained terraced gardens, and cultivated a variety of crops, including cucumbers, bananas, sweet potatoes, beans, and tobacco.

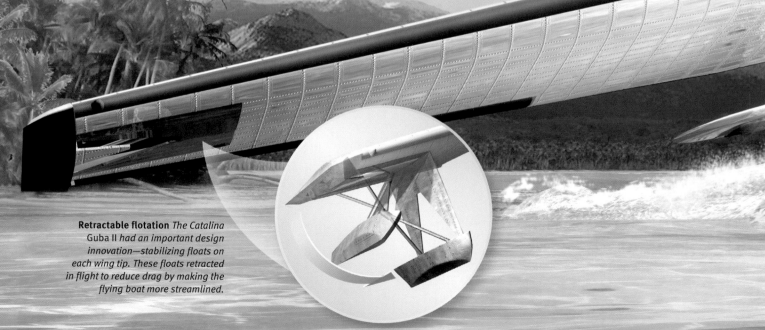

Retractable flotation *The Catalina Guba II had an important design innovation—stabilizing floats on each wing tip. These floats retracted in flight to reduce drag by making the flying boat more streamlined.*

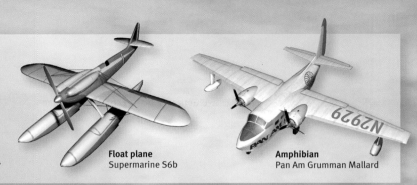

Different seaplanes
The Supermarine S6b—a float plane—won the Schneider Cup for Great Britain in 1931. The Grumman Mallard is an amphibious seaplane and can take off and land on airfields and water. Its fuselage serves as the key means for flotation.

Float plane
Supermarine S6b

Amphibian
Pan Am Grumman Mallard

Engines *The* Guba II *was an early version of the Catalina design, equipped with two Pratt & Whitney engines. They were mounted on the leading edge of the parasol wing.*

Parasol wing *The Catalina* Guba II *had a distinctive parasol wing, which was supported by streamlined struts on both sides of the fuselage. The raised wing helped prevent water from spraying onto the engines.*

Wing strut

Viewing area *An observation deck was housed in the nose section of the Guba II. From this position, it was easy to spot river or lake landing sites.*

Entrance hatch
Passengers, crew, and cargo moved in and out of the flying boat through the entrance hatch. A panel in the rear fuselage gave further access for cargo.

GUBA

F/A-18 HORNET: THE FACTS

LENGTH:	55.8 feet (17 m)
WINGSPAN:	37.4 feet (11.4 m)
WEIGHT:	24,691.8 pounds (11,200 kg)
ENGINE:	Two General Electric F404-400 turbofans
CREW AND PASSENGERS:	One pilot

Swift attacker

Flying from the deck of the USS *Nimitz*, an F/A-18 Hornet leaves on a night mission. The fast and well-armed aircraft can arrive quickly at a potential or real war zone. The aircraft carrier serves as an air base at sea. The flight deck becomes the center for action with aircraft of many types landing and taking off—all in a very limited space.

F/A-18
Hornet

The F/A-18 Hornet is an all-weather and multipurpose fighter. For decades, the US Navy has used the Hornet for aircraft carrier duty. The Navy's top aerobatic demonstration team, the Blue Angels, has flown the Hornet since 1986. But the Hornet is designed for the role of a "strike fighter." It is a single-seat fighter that can attack targets on land and in the air. The F/A-18 played a dramatic role in the Gulf War of 1990–1991, destroying enemy aircraft and bombing key targets. In 2002, the advanced F/A-18 Super Hornet began service on the carrier USS *Abraham Lincoln*. It is larger, has more powerful engines, and better weapon technology. In 2003, the Super Hornet took part in the lead-up to the Iraq War. The F/A-18 is one of the best all-around fighters in the world.

Island *This structure houses the primary flight control deck, where the commander of aircraft and his crew control flight operations.*

Arresting wires *Four arresting wires are stretched across the deck. They are spaced at 50-foot (15-m) intervals.*

Jet blast deflector *Retractable steel walls deflect the jet exhaust away from the deck.*

AIRCRAFT CATAPULT

A catapult can propel an airplane from zero to 165 miles per hour (266 km/h) in two seconds. The holdback secures the plane as its engines start to generate thrust. Steam pressure builds up in the cylinder. When it reaches high pressure, it releases the holdback and forces the pistons and aircraft forward down the runway. The pulley and cable pull the pistons back to start position.

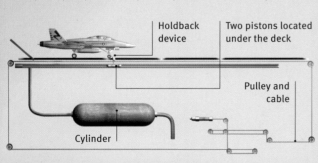

Holdback device

Two pistons located under the deck

Pulley and cable

Cylinder

Catapult tracks

TOP SPEED

2,170 mph (3,500 km/h)

1,860 mph (3,000 km/h)

1,550 mph (2,500 km/h)

Hornet 1,190 mph (1,915 km/h)

930 mph (1,500 km/h)

Mach 1

620 mph (1,000 km/h)

310 mph (500 km/h)

0

Wings extended *The F/A-18 Hornet is a delta wing design. When it is on the carrier, the wings can be folded up for storage and moving around.*

Missiles *Each F/A-18 can carry a variety of weapons including an 0.8-inch (20-mm) cannon, air-to-air missiles, air-to-ground missiles, and laser-guided bombs.*

Flight controls *The Hornet has advanced electronic systems. The cockpit displays are computerized, and it has a digital fly-by-wire flight control system.*

Safety net

Limited landing
Landing on an aircraft carrier is a very difficult task. The runway is only 500 feet (152 m) long. Each plane has a tailhook that catches an arresting wire on the flight deck. This stops the forward movement of the plane.

The pilot drops the tailhook and aims to catch the third arresting wire stretched across the flight deck.

The aircraft lands at 150 miles per hour (241 km/h), but comes to a halt in two seconds after catching the wire.

F-117A NIGHTHAWK: THE FACTS

LENGTH: **63.6 feet (19.4 m)**

WINGSPAN: **43.3 feet (13.2 m)**

WEIGHT: **52,500 pounds (23,625 kg)**

ENGINE: **Two General Electric F404 turbofans**

CREW AND PASSENGERS: **One pilot**

V-tail *The distinctive v-tail has two movable control surfaces, which serve as elevators, rudders, and ailerons. They are often called "ruddervons" to explain their combined function.*

F-117A
Nighthawk

Difficult to detect or track by radar, the F-117A Nighthawk first demonstrated modern stealth aircraft technology in the Gulf War of 1991. In 1998, the Nighthawk was used in the Kosovo war. The futuristic design of the aircraft came from the top-secret "black" weapons program of the United States in the Cold War. On night missions, the F-117A flew as a ghostly and deadly presence over enemy territory. It could strike targets suddenly with laser-guided bombs. A single-seat aircraft, the Nighthawk is equipped with advanced navigation and weapons systems, including the latest digital fly-by-wire flight controls. Now retired from operational service, the F-117A is remembered as a pathfinder in stealth technology.

Jet nozzles *Wide, flat jet nozzles reduce and disperse exhaust. This function is essential to avoid infrared missiles.*

Unmanned spy plane

By the start of the twenty-first century, the US Air Force had introduced a number of Unmanned Aerial Vehicles (UAV) to serve as spy planes. The Global Hawk UAV, with a wingspan of 115 feet (35 m), can collect data at altitudes of 65,000 feet (19,800 m) and has no pilot on board.

Satellite in head

Outer skin *The F-117A has an outer skin coated with radar-absorbing materials to avoid enemy radar and infrared sensors.*

TOP SPEED

2,170 mph (3,500 km/h)

1,860 mph (3,000 km/h)

1,550 mph (2,500 km/h)

1,240 mph (2,000 km/h)

930 mph (1,500 km/h)

Mach 1

Nighthawk 617 mph (993 km/h)

310 mph (500 km/h)

0

Undetectable aircraft

The F-117A is a "low-observable" aircraft. It is hard to detect because of its stealth properties. These are its computer-generated wing and fuselage design, angular shape, and outer skin coated with radar-absorbing materials. The F-117A is fitted with an internal weapons store with a payload that includes two laser-guided bombs. Newer versions of the aircraft use satellite guidance to strike the enemy through bad weather and smoke to trick and avoid enemy missiles.

AVOIDING RADAR DETECTION

The Nighthawk is designed to reduce any chance of detection by the enemy. The cockpit is angled to deflect radar signals. Sensors, antennae, and weaponry are hidden in the fuselage. Inlets to the jet engines are covered with fine screens to conceal the engine turbines.

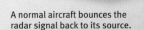

A normal aircraft bounces the radar signal back to its source.

A stealth aircraft bounces radar in many directions and only an amount equal to that of an insect returns to the source.

Cockpit *The windows are flat and framed by heavy metal partitions. They sit on a pyramid-style dome. The window edges are serrated and deflect radar.*

Infrared sensor *Below the forward cockpit windshield is the "forward-looking infrared" sensor (FLIR). This rotating infrared detector is used to spot targets.*

Smart bombs *The first operational F-117A was armed with two GBU-27 laser-guided bombs— a load of 4,000 pounds (1,800 kg) in weight.*

Engine air intake *Engine air inlets have grids to disperse enemy radar.*

Forward-faceted tubes *The Nighthawk has four probes, or extensions, on the nose section. These probes gather essential flight data.*

TOP SPEED

| 0 | 310 mph (500 km/h) | 620 mph (1,000 km/h) | 930 mph (1,500 km/h) | Mach 1 | 1,240 mph (2,000 km/h) | F-22 1,500 mph (2,414 km/h) | 1,860 mph (3,000 km/h) | 2,170 mph (3,500 km/h) |

Radar system *The onboard radar system has a transmitter that changes its wave frequency more than 1,000 times a second to avoid enemy detection.*

Head-up display (HUD)
The pilot uses a head-up display. Information is projected onto the cockpit screen so that the pilot does not have to look down. Pilots also use helmet-up displays—they can view data on their visor.

Frameless cockpit *The Raptor has one of the first all-glass cockpits for a modern fighter. The large frameless canopy is made of clear polycarbonate plastic.*

Clipped delta wing *The wing design of the F-22 is called a "clipped delta" type. This design improves efficiency at high speeds. The Raptor's wings also contain the fuel tanks.*

F-22 RAPTOR: THE FACTS

LENGTH: 62 feet (18.9 m)

WINGSPAN: 44.6 feet (13.6 m)

WEIGHT: 43,431 pounds (19,700 kg)

ENGINE: Two Pratt & Whitney F119-PW-100

CREW AND PASSENGERS: One pilot

F-22
Raptor

The F-22 Raptor is a new supersonic fighter plane. It is an impressive mix of stealth, speed, and maneuverability. It was introduced for military action in 2005, and its design makes it hard to detect or shoot down. Its engines enable it to fly at around Mach 1.7. It also has a "supercruise" option and can fly at supersonic speeds for long periods without the use of afterburners, which use a lot of fuel. The fighter is equipped with an array of weapons, including an 0.8-inch (20-mm) cannon and an onboard store of precision missiles and bombs. The pilot launches these weapons from hidden positions in the wing and fuselage. The Raptor can fly to a maximum altitude of 60,000 feet (18,300 m).

Supercruiser

The F-22 Raptor is able to cruise at supersonic speeds. While flying at 30,000 feet (9,000 m), the pilot can cruise at 1,070 miles per hour (1,725 km/h). He can quickly direct his aircraft skyward to fly at 50,000 feet (15,240 m) for a more exhilarating ride. Many of the Raptor's computer-based systems are kept secret by governments, or are "classified."

SUPERSONIC WING SHAPES

Aircraft designers are always searching for new wing shapes to increase the speed of supersonic planes.

Delta wing, Mirage 111 AO, 1956

Swing wing, Tupolev Tu-26, 1984

Sweepback wing, Super Etendard, 1974

Short thin wing, F-104 Starfighter, 1954

Forward-swept wing, Grumman X-29A, 1984

Tail fin *The tail of the Raptor has a distinctive "V" shape. The design improves control and the stealth properties of the aircraft.*

Movable nozzle *The Raptor's engines are fitted with the world's first "vectoring" nozzles. These nozzles, at the rear of the engine, can move up and down, which increases the plane's maneuverability.*

F119 twin engines *Two powerful jet engines enable the Raptor to cruise at supersonic speeds. The engines can produce 35,000 pounds (15,900 kg) of thrust.*

2,170 mph
(3,500 km/h)

1,860 mph
(3,000 km/h)

1,550 mph
(2,500 km/h)

1,240 mph
(2,000 km/h)

930 mph
(1,500 km/h)

Mach 1

A320 561 mph
(903 km/h)

310 mph
(500 km/h)

0

AIRBUS A320: THE FACTS
LENGTH: 123 feet (37.6 m)

WINGSPAN: 111.9 feet (34.1 m)

WEIGHT: 93,079 pounds (42,220 kg)

ENGINE: Two CFMI CFM56-5 or two IAE V2500

CREW AND PASSENGERS: Two crew in the cockpit; four flight
attendants and up to 150 passengers

On the Tarmac
Airbus A320

The Airbus A320 is a typical modern commercial
airliner with seating for 150 passengers. The
streamlined A320, launched in 1984, was the first
airliner to use a fly-by-wire flight control system—
an electronic instead of a mechanical and hydraulic
system. This advanced computer-controlled technology
operated in a new-style glass cockpit with several
colored computer display screens. The pilot had
"sidestick" controllers to fly and steer the aircraft.
The A320 features two powerful turbofan engines.
Each engine can generate up to 26,500 pounds
(12,000 kg) of thrust. These engines, located on
each wing, are very quiet during flights.

Quick changeover
Passengers do not usually get to see
the many technicians and cleaners on the
ground, who are essential for commercial
flight operations. A large group of highly
trained ground staff is needed to refuel and
clean the plane, load cargo and luggage,
and maintain the A320 flight systems.

Refueling nozzle *Modern
airliners use enormous
amounts of aviation fuel.
Refueling requires strict
safety procedures. A large
refueling nozzle is
carefully connected to the
airliner's fuel tanks.*

Fuel-transfer vehicle
*This pumps aviation fuel
from underground tanks
into the aircraft tanks.*

Mobile stairs *Mobile
and retractable stairs
allow ground staff to
access the cabin.*

Toilet-waste truck
*This removes all toilet
waste from the aircraft.*

Emptying toilets
*All airliners use a vacuum
toilet system. To service
the toilets, the ground
crew uses a special truck
with a suction pump that
connects to the onboard
vacuum toilet tank.*

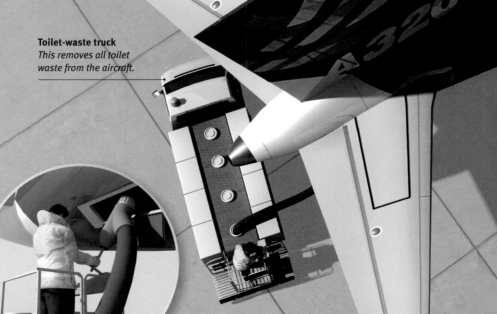

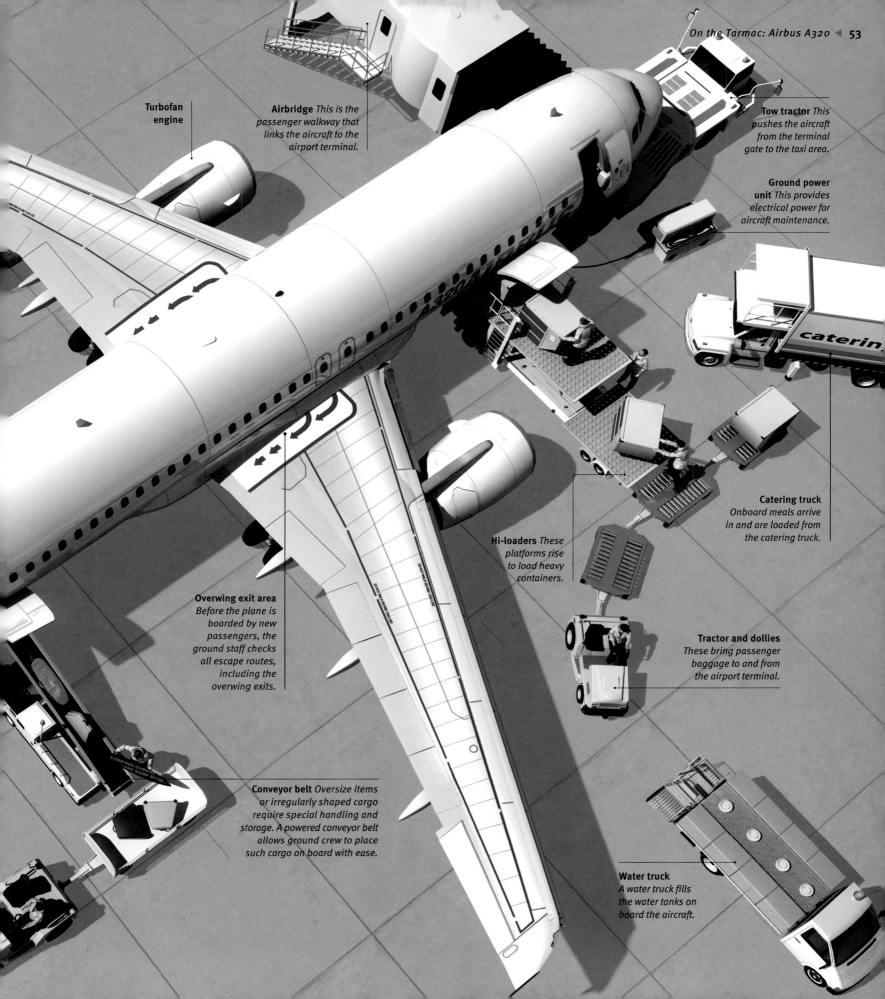

Turbofan engine

Airbridge *This is the passenger walkway that links the aircraft to the airport terminal.*

Tow tractor *This pushes the aircraft from the terminal gate to the taxi area.*

Ground power unit *This provides electrical power for aircraft maintenance.*

Catering truck *Onboard meals arrive in and are loaded from the catering truck.*

Hi-loaders *These platforms rise to load heavy containers.*

Tractor and dollies *These bring passenger baggage to and from the airport terminal.*

Overwing exit area *Before the plane is boarded by new passengers, the ground staff checks all escape routes, including the overwing exits.*

Conveyor belt *Oversize items or irregularly shaped cargo require special handling and storage. A powered conveyor belt allows ground crew to place such cargo on board with ease.*

Water truck *A water truck fills the water tanks on board the aircraft.*

HOW DOES A HELICOPTER FLY?

A helicopter's rotor, the set of spinning blades, provides a lift force for flight. It is connected to collective pitch and cyclic pitch levers, which the pilot uses to control the helicopter. The small tail rotor holds the helicopter in a straight line while ascending, descending, flying forward, and flying sideways.

Up and down By raising the blue collective pitch lever the helicopter goes upward, and to go down the blue lever is lowered.

Flying around The yellow cyclic pitch lever controls forward thrust and sideways movement.

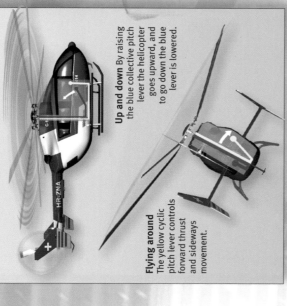

Main rotor *The main rotor is the set of spinning wings that produce lift for the helicopter to fly. It is also essential to controlling the helicopter.*

EUROCOPTER EC 145: THE FACTS

LENGTH: 42.7 feet (13 m)

BLADE LENGTH: 42.7 feet (13 m)

WEIGHT: 3,951 pounds (1,792 kg)

ENGINE: Two Turbomeca Arriel 1E2 turboshafts

CREW: One pilot; nine passengers

Eurocopter EC 145
Helicopter

The creation of a flying machine that lifted effortlessly from the ground, hovered, then landed safely seemed impossible for centuries. Around 1500, famed inventor Leonardo da Vinci proposed the first helicopter-type design, but it was not until 1939 that Russian–American designer Igor Sikorsky built and flew the VS–300, arguably the first practical helicopter. Since then, helicopters have been essential in commercial air transport. They were first deployed by the military in World War II and performed a vital role in the Vietnam War. The Eurocopter EC 145, a twin-engine utility helicopter, is widely known today for its high-profile role in rescue work. Along with other modern helicopters, it serves in medical emergencies, shuttle services, traffic control, and civilian transport.

Tail rotor *This rotor steers the helicopter and prevents it from spinning in the opposite direction of the main rotor.*

| TOP SPEED | 0 | Eurocopter EC 145 153 mph (246 km/h) | 310 mph (500 km/h) | 620 mph (1,000 km/h) | 930 mph (1,500 km/h) | 1,240 mph (2,000 km/h) | Mach 1 | 1,550 mph (2,500 km/h) | 1,860 mph (3,000 km/h) | 2,170 mph (3,500 km/h) |

Rescue device *The electrically powered rescue hoist can hold up to 595 pounds (270 kg) and has a 295-foot- (90-m-) long cable. It is essential for rescue operations, especially in heavily wooded areas or at sea.*

Highly skilled hovering

The pilot of the Swiss Air Rescue Eurocopter EC 145 hovers, while the winch operator lowers down to haul a rescue aboard. Hovering is difficult in the face of crosswinds—the pilot must delicately handle the collective, cyclic, and rudder controls to maintain a fixed position. It is a little like trying to pat your head and rub your stomach while balancing on a bowling ball.

Tiltrotor technology

A tiltrotor uses its rotors to take off or land vertically, like a helicopter. It then tilts its rotors and moves forward. The tilt rotors operate as normal propellers so the aircraft flies like an airplane.

Takeoff Rotors spin to create upward movement like a helicopter.

Tilted Rotors are tilted for desired direction or movement.

Forward Rotors are in a horizontal position for forward movement, like a plane.

ZEPPELIN NT: THE FACTS

LENGTH:	246 feet (75 m)
HEIGHT:	57 feet (17.4 m)
WEIGHT:	17,688 pounds (8,040 kg)
ENGINE:	Three Lycoming 10-360 197 hp (147 kW) engines
CREW AND PASSENGERS:	Two pilots; 12 passengers

Modern Airship

Zeppelin NT

An airship flies with the aid of a lifting gas, such as hot air, hydrogen, or helium, and is propelled forward by an engine. In 1901, Alberto Santos-Dumont, a Brazilian air enthusiast, developed the first practical airship—a motorized, lighter-than-air flying machine. His breakthrough set the stage for a new form of flying. Two types of craft evolved: non-rigid airships (blimps) and rigid airships (dirigibles). Dirigibles were often called Zeppelins in honor of Ferdinand Graf von Zeppelin who pioneered them for use in war and peace. In the 1920s and 1930s, airships carried thousands of passengers around the globe. Airships and dirigibles are still used today, mainly for advertising, tourism, and research. The Zeppelin NT (New Technology) is one example of renewed interest in dirigibles.

Inside the hangar

A modern Zeppelin hangar houses two airships: one under construction (right), the other being serviced (below). Outside the hangar, another airship can be seen in flight. The Zeppelin NT is known for its great maneuverability; the pilot can tilt the two front engines up to 120 degrees and the rear engine up to 90 degrees.

In flight *A third Zeppelin NT flies above the airship hangar. Clearly visible is the gondola of the airship, which seats 12 passengers comfortably. Such an airship may cruise at speeds up to 78 miles per hour (126 km/h).*

In transit *A second airship enters the hangar to be serviced. It is pulled by a special tow truck, then secured by a tie-down link from the nose section. The ground crew can then move the airship into the hangar without difficulty.*

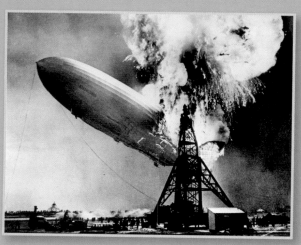

Hindenburg disaster

In 1936, the *Hindenburg* flew more than 1,300 people from Germany to the USA. Tragedy struck in 1937 when the airship burst into flames while landing at Lakehurst, New Jersey. The accident killed 35 passengers and marked the end of commercial airship service.

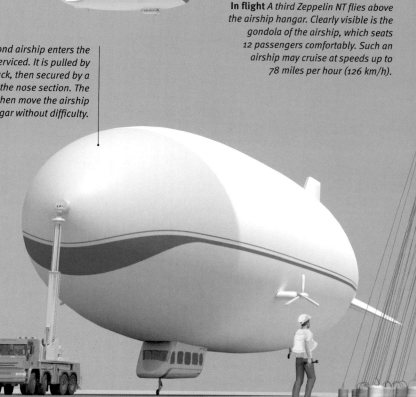

TOP SPEED

2,170 mph (3,500 km/h)	
1,860 mph (3,000 km/h)	
1,550 mph (2,500 km/h)	
1,240 mph (2,000 km/h)	
930 mph (1,500 km/h)	
Mach 1	
620 mph (1,000 km/h)	
Zeppelin NT 78 mph (125 km/h)	
0	

Two types of airship

Airships are rigid or non-rigid. Rigid airships have a fixed skeletal structure within an envelope. Non-rigid blimps maintain their structure by the pressure of contained gas. Both types use engines for propulsion and use the flying technology of airplanes.

The giant *Graf Zeppelin* of the 1920s (rigid dirigible)

Non-rigid airship (blimp)

Envelope *A three-layered laminate envelope is pulled over the metal frame. Inside the envelope, two large bags are inflated with helium. The noncombustible helium gas provides excellent lift.*

Frame *The inner rigid framework of the Zeppelin NT is fixed and durable. It consists of large aluminum beams and carbon-fiber trusses, or cross sections.*

310 mph (500 km/h)	620 mph (1,000 km/h)	Mach 1	930 mph (1,500 km/h)	1,240 mph (2,000 km/h)	1,550 mph (2,500 km/h)	1,860 mph (3,000 km/h)	SpaceShipOne 2,186 mph (3,518 km/h)

Flying cars

The creation of a futuristic flying car is an old dream. Some people believe a flying car that can take off and land vertically, hover, and fly at subsonic speeds could become a reality in the twenty-first century.

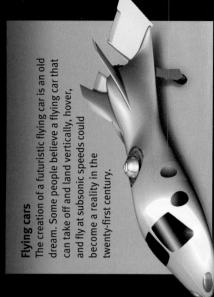

SPACESHIPONE: THE FACTS

LENGTH: 28 feet (8.5 m)

WINGSPAN: 27 feet (8.2 m)

WEIGHT : 2,645 pounds (1,200 kg)

ENGINE (ROCKET): One SpaceDev SD010 Hybrid Motor

CREW AND PASSENGERS: One pilot; two crew

Into the Future

SpaceShipOne

The futuristic SpaceShipOne won the Ansari X Prize in 2004—a multimillion-dollar prize for the first civilian spacecraft to cross the border from Earth's atmosphere into outer space. SpaceShipOne rocketed to the towering altitude of 69.6 miles (112 km), breaking the existing record established in the 1960s by the rocket-powered X-15 plane. SpaceShipOne was air-launched at 50,000 feet (15,240 m) from the carrier ship *White Knight* and then flown manually to the edge of outer space, leaving only a trail of white smoke. After all the fuel burned out, the pilot had about 3.5 minutes of zero gravity and time to look into the black of outer space. The entire flight took about 30 minutes.

Return journey

After reaching outer space, the pilot prepares SpaceShipOne for reentry into Earth's atmosphere. The pilot slows the aircraft to keep the outside surfaces from overheating. By pushing two levers, the pilot flips the twin rear stabilizers into a vertical position, creating a "feathering" effect. The descent is at a fairly slow speed—178 miles per hour (287 km/h). By slowing down, the spacecraft avoids some overheating, so only one-fifth of the external surfaces require thermal protection. Finally, the tail is raised for the glide home to land.

Space station *In the future, a space station could be a docking facility for spacecraft and provide hotel accommodation for space tourists.*

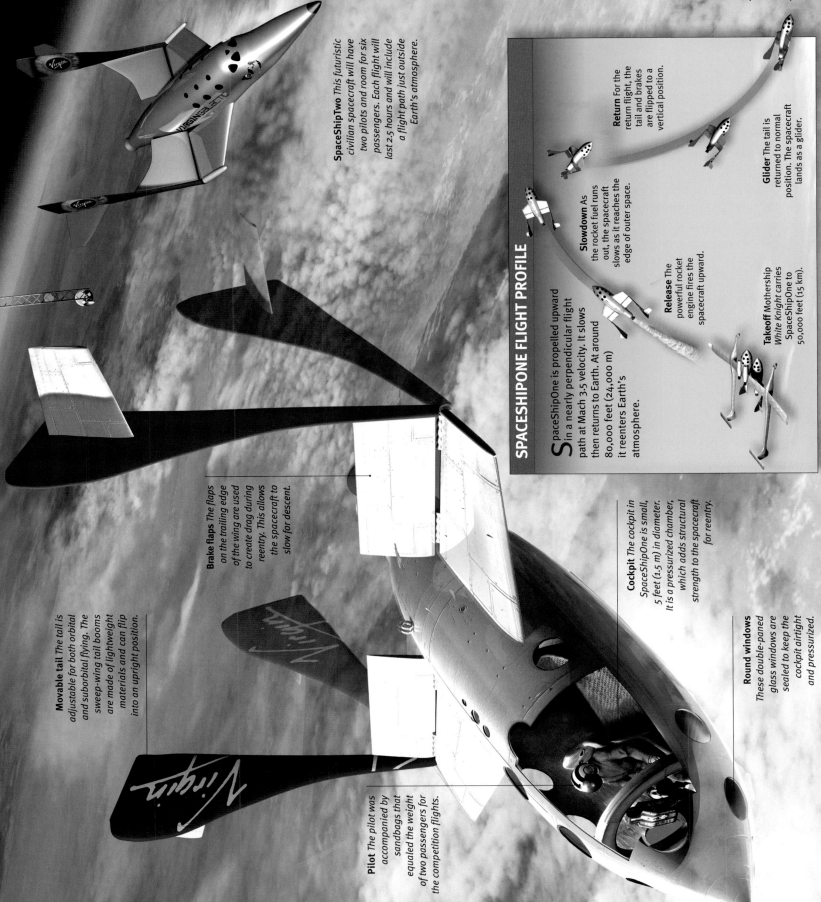

SpaceShipTwo This futuristic civilian spacecraft will have two pilots and room for six passengers. Each flight will last 2.5 hours and will include a flight path just outside Earth's atmosphere.

Movable tail The tail is adjustable for both orbital and suborbital flying. The sweep-wing tail booms are made of lightweight materials and can flip into an upright position.

Brake flaps The flaps on the trailing edge of the wing are used to create drag during reentry. This allows the spacecraft to slow for descent.

Pilot The pilot was accompanied by sandbags that equaled the weight of two passengers for the competition flights.

Cockpit The cockpit in SpaceShipOne is small, 5 feet (1.5 m) in diameter. It is a pressurized chamber, which adds structural strength to the spacecraft for reentry.

Round windows These double-paned glass windows are sealed to keep the cockpit airtight and pressurized.

SPACESHIPONE FLIGHT PROFILE

SpaceShipOne is propelled upward in a nearly perpendicular flight path at Mach 3.5 velocity. It slows then returns to Earth. At around 80,000 feet (24,000 m) it reenters Earth's atmosphere.

Return For the return flight, the tail and brakes are flipped to a vertical position.

Glider The tail is returned to normal position. The spacecraft lands as a glider.

Slowdown As the rocket fuel runs out, the spacecraft slows as it reaches the edge of outer space.

Release The powerful rocket engine fires the spacecraft upward.

Takeoff Mothership White Knight carries SpaceShipOne to 50,000 feet (15 km).

Flight Facts

CONTROLLED FLIGHT

An airplane can rotate in three different ways: pitch, roll, and yaw. They determine the attitude or position of the aircraft while it is in motion through the airstream.

Pitch Movement of the nose of the aircraft upward or downward is called "pitch."

Roll The wing ailerons control the "roll," or "bank," right or left of the aircraft.

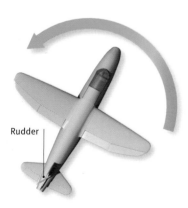

Yaw The pilot controls nose left or right, or "yaw," with the rudder on the tail.

CONTROL SURFACES

The Wright brothers first achieved flight with control in 1903. Modern airplanes are fitted with ailerons, elevators, and the rudder, which redirect the airstream and allow the pilot to maintain direction and altitude in flight.

Spoilers/airbrakes
These help reduce altitude without losing speed. They enable a plane to slow down rapidly for landing.

Elevators
The elevators are on the tail and control the pitch of the plane.

Flaps
On the edge of the wing, the flaps help the aircraft to gain more lift at slower speeds.

Rudder
The rudder controls the yaw of the plane. It is located on the vertical stabilizer on the tail.

Ailerons
The ailerons move in opposite directions from each other and control the aircraft roll.

Slats
The slats on the front of the wing are often retractable and increase lift, especially during takeoff and landing.

FAMOUS FLIGHTS

The progress of aviation has been marked by the achievements of many pioneers determined to dominate the skies. The twentieth century was filled with exciting aviation firsts, some of which are listed here.

The Bell X-1 broke the sound barrier in 1947.

Year	Famous First Flight	Aircraft	Pilot
1903	Powered and controlled flight	Flyer	Wright brothers
1909	Flight over the English Channel	Blériot XI	Louis Blériot
1912	First woman to fly over the English Channel	Blériot XI	Harriet Quimby
1914	Round-trip from St. Petersburg to Kiev	*Il'ya Muromets*	Igor Sikorsky
1927	First transatlantic flight	*Spirit of St. Louis*	Charles Lindbergh
1928	First flight across the Pacific	Fokker F.VIIb-3M *Southern Cross*	Charles Kingsford-Smith and Charles T. P. Ulm
1929	First around-the-world airship flight	*Graf Zeppelin*	Hugo Eckener
1931	London, UK, to Darwin, Australia	DH.60G Gypsy Moth *Jason*	Amy Johnson
1947	Breaking the sound barrier	Bell X-1	Charles E. Yeager
1953	First woman to fly Mach 1	F-86	Jacqueline Cochran
1986	First around-the-world plane flight	Voyager	Dick Rutan and Jeana Yeager
1999	First around-the-world balloon flight	Orbiter 3	Bertrand Piccard and Brian Jones
2004	First civilian aircraft in outer space	SpaceShipOne	Brian Binnie

PARADE OF AIRCRAFT

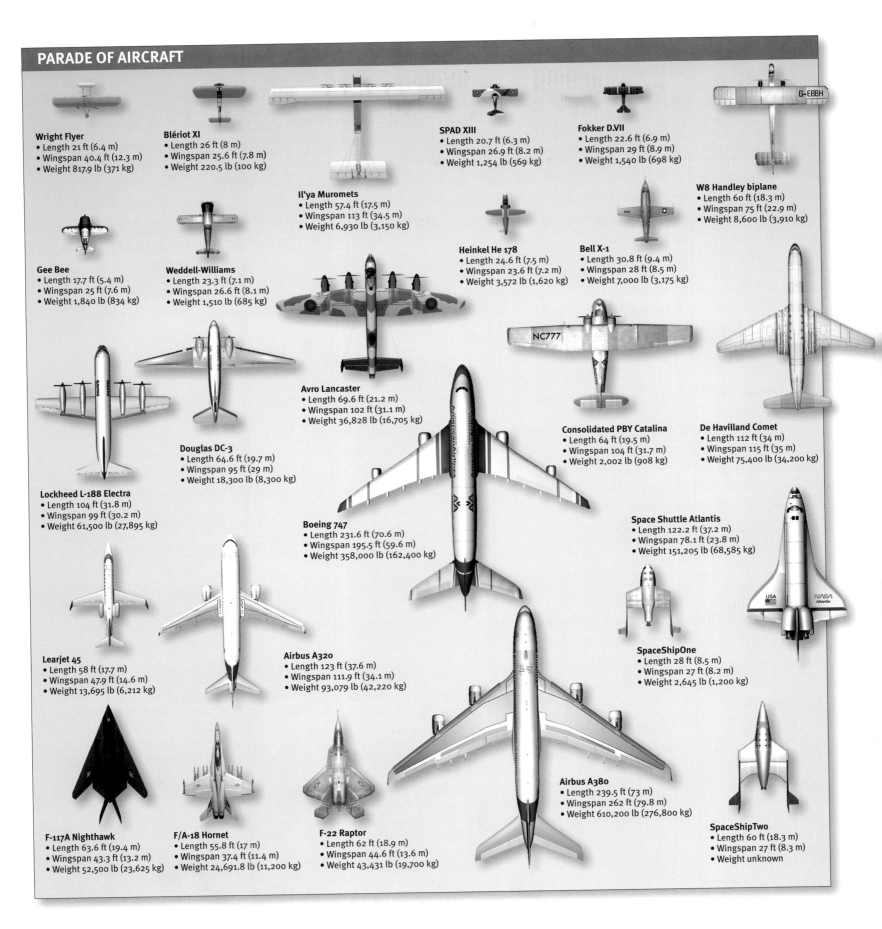

Wright Flyer
- Length 21 ft (6.4 m)
- Wingspan 40.4 ft (12.3 m)
- Weight 817.9 lb (371 kg)

Blériot XI
- Length 26 ft (8 m)
- Wingspan 25.6 ft (7.8 m)
- Weight 220.5 lb (100 kg)

Il'ya Muromets
- Length 57.4 ft (17.5 m)
- Wingspan 113 ft (34.5 m)
- Weight 6,930 lb (3,150 kg)

SPAD XIII
- Length 20.7 ft (6.3 m)
- Wingspan 26.9 ft (8.2 m)
- Weight 1,254 lb (569 kg)

Fokker D.VII
- Length 22.6 ft (6.9 m)
- Wingspan 29 ft (8.9 m)
- Weight 1,540 lb (698 kg)

W8 Handley biplane
- Length 60 ft (18.3 m)
- Wingspan 75 ft (22.9 m)
- Weight 8,600 lb (3,910 kg)

Gee Bee
- Length 17.7 ft (5.4 m)
- Wingspan 25 ft (7.6 m)
- Weight 1,840 lb (834 kg)

Weddell-Williams
- Length 23.3 ft (7.1 m)
- Wingspan 26.6 ft (8.1 m)
- Weight 1,510 lb (685 kg)

Heinkel He 178
- Length 24.6 ft (7.5 m)
- Wingspan 23.6 ft (7.2 m)
- Weight 3,572 lb (1,620 kg)

Bell X-1
- Length 30.8 ft (9.4 m)
- Wingspan 28 ft (8.5 m)
- Weight 7,000 lb (3,175 kg)

Avro Lancaster
- Length 69.6 ft (21.2 m)
- Wingspan 102 ft (31.1 m)
- Weight 36,828 lb (16,705 kg)

Douglas DC-3
- Length 64.6 ft (19.7 m)
- Wingspan 95 ft (29 m)
- Weight 18,300 lb (8,300 kg)

Consolidated PBY Catalina
- Length 64 ft (19.5 m)
- Wingspan 104 ft (31.7 m)
- Weight 2,002 lb (908 kg)

De Havilland Comet
- Length 112 ft (34 m)
- Wingspan 115 ft (35 m)
- Weight 75,400 lb (34,200 kg)

Lockheed L-188 Electra
- Length 104 ft (31.8 m)
- Wingspan 99 ft (30.2 m)
- Weight 61,500 lb (27,895 kg)

Boeing 747
- Length 231.6 ft (70.6 m)
- Wingspan 195.5 ft (59.6 m)
- Weight 358,000 lb (162,400 kg)

Space Shuttle Atlantis
- Length 122.2 ft (37.2 m)
- Wingspan 78.1 ft (23.8 m)
- Weight 151,205 lb (68,585 kg)

Learjet 45
- Length 58 ft (17.7 m)
- Wingspan 47.9 ft (14.6 m)
- Weight 13,695 lb (6,212 kg)

Airbus A320
- Length 123 ft (37.6 m)
- Wingspan 111.9 ft (34.1 m)
- Weight 93,079 lb (42,220 kg)

SpaceShipOne
- Length 28 ft (8.5 m)
- Wingspan 27 ft (8.2 m)
- Weight 2,645 lb (1,200 kg)

F-117A Nighthawk
- Length 63.6 ft (19.4 m)
- Wingspan 43.3 ft (13.2 m)
- Weight 52,500 lb (23,625 kg)

F/A-18 Hornet
- Length 55.8 ft (17 m)
- Wingspan 37.4 ft (11.4 m)
- Weight 24,691.8 lb (11,200 kg)

F-22 Raptor
- Length 62 ft (18.9 m)
- Wingspan 44.6 ft (13.6 m)
- Weight 43,431 lb (19,700 kg)

Airbus A380
- Length 239.5 ft (73 m)
- Wingspan 262 ft (79.8 m)
- Weight 610,200 lb (276,800 kg)

SpaceShipTwo
- Length 60 ft (18.3 m)
- Wingspan 27 ft (8.3 m)
- Weight unknown

Glossary

aerodynamics The science that deals with air and how aircraft fly.

aerodyne A term for aircraft that get their lift in flight mainly from aerodynamic forces.

ailerons Movable controls that are fixed to the wings of airplanes and are used to make an airplane bank, or roll.

airflow The flow of air past a moving aircraft.

airfoil A structure such as a wing, a tailplane, or a propeller blade that develops lift when moving quickly through air.

airplane A powered, heavier-than-air aircraft.

airship Lighter-than-air aircraft that is driven by an engine and able to be steered.

altitude An aviation term for height.

amphibian A type of seaplane that can take off and land on airfields or water.

angle of attack The angle at which the wing meets the airstream.

area rule A special way of designing the shape of an airplane to reduce drag when it flies at supersonic speeds.

ATC (Air Traffic Control) The means to separate and control the movement of aircraft in flight and for takeoff and landing at airports.

autogiro A type of rotor airplane that gets lift from rotating airfoils.

autopilot An automatic control mechanism that keeps an airplane in level flight and on a set course chosen by the pilot.

balloon An unsteerable aircraft that is lighter than air.

balloon basket This holds the pilot, passengers, and flight instruments.

bank When the pilot lowers one wing and raises the other during a turn.

biplane A fixed-wing airplane with two sets of wings.

catapult A powerful, steam-powered device that launches airplanes from an aircraft carrier or ship.

cockpit The open or closed compartment where the pilot and/or crew sit to fly the aircraft.

collective pitch The control that makes a helicopter climb and descend.

controlled air space Where air traffic control procedures regulate the flight of aircraft in a certain zone or region.

cyclic pitch The control that makes a helicopter move in a horizontal direction.

drag The resistance caused by the shape of an aircraft to its movement through air.

ejection seat A rocket-powered seat that launches, or ejects, the pilot out of an airplane. The pilot then parachutes to safety.

elevator A movable control attached to the tailplane that makes an airplane climb or descend.

fin The fixed, vertical part of the tail unit that helps keep an airplane flying straight ahead. Also called the vertical stabilizer.

float plane A seaplane that is supported on water by floats.

fly-by-wire system A modern form of flight control where electric wiring replaces mechanical or hydraulic links to ailerons, flaps, and rudder of the aircraft.

flying boat A seaplane that is supported on water by its fuselage.

fuselage The main or core body of an aircraft.

gas burners Burners that are fed by propane gas to provide the heat that lifts a hot air balloon.

glass cockpit An aircraft cockpit that uses electronic instruments, such as computers, instead of traditional mechanical gauges.

glider An unpowered, heavier-than-air aircraft.

gondola The passenger and crew cabin of an airship.

helicopter An aircraft that gets its lift from a powered rotor.

IFR (Instrument Flight Rules) Rules of the road for flying by instruments in clouds and low visibility conditions.

ILS (Instrument Landing System) A system that uses radio beams and marker lighting to precisely guide an aircraft's final approach to landing.

infrared missiles Rocket-powered missiles that are guided to their target by an infrared homing system. They detect objects in a way that is similar to the automatic focusing system used on many automatic cameras.

jet stream A narrow band of high-altitude winds exceeding 100 miles per hour (160 km/h).

joy flight When people pay to fly in a small airplane to experience the excitement of flying.

kite A tethered glider that is lifted by the wind. A kite was the first heavier-than-air aircraft.

landing gear The name for the wheels that support an airplane on the ground. It is also called the undercarriage.

lift The upward force created when the airstream passes around an airfoil, such as a wing, a tailplane, or a propeller blade.

Mach number A measurement for speeds in excess of the speed of sound. Mach 1.0 is the speed of sound. A plane that flies at Mach 2.0 is flying at twice the speed of sound.

monoplane A fixed-wing airplane with one set of wings.

orbit To circle Earth, another planet, or a star in space.

pitch The aerodynamic term used to describe an airplane's nose moving up and down.

primary feathers A bird's outermost wing feathers that provide the thrust for flight.

propeller A set of blades driven by an engine that pull or push an airplane through air. It is sometimes called an airscrew.

pylon racing Air racing close to the ground around a course marked by painted pylons.

radar A method of using radio beams for navigation or to show other objects in the air.

reconnaissance plane A military aircraft designed for air observation over enemy territory. Reconnaissance aircraft may be used for visual observation or photography.

roll The aerodynamic term used to describe an airplane banking.

rotors Two or more long narrow wings, called blades, that provide lift for a helicopter or an autogiro.

rudder A movable control fixed to the fin that helps control direction.

sailplane A high-performance glider designed specially to soar on thermals or rising air.

sonic boom A sound like a thunderclap that is caused from the shock waves of a passing supersonic aircraft.

sound barrier An invisible, aerodynamic "barrier" that was once thought to limit the speed of an aircraft. Aircraft encounter extreme buffeting as they approach the speed of sound.

space shuttle A reusable spacecraft used for travel into and near Earth's orbits.

speed of sound At high altitudes, this is 662 miles per hour (1,065 km/h); at sea level the speed of sound is 760 miles per hour (1,223 km/h).

stability A plane needs to be stable when it flies. Its wings, fuselage, and tailplanes make it easy, safe, and smooth to fly.

stall This happens when there is a breakdown of the airflow over the airfoil or wing, which results in an abrupt loss of lift.

streamlining The design of wings and fuselage with smooth surfaces in order to reduce air resistance or drag.

subsonic Flying at speeds less than the speed of sound.

supersonic Flying faster than the speed of sound.

tailplane The fixed, horizontal part of the tail unit that helps to keep an airplane stable. Also called the horizontal stabilizer.

thermal A column of rising air used by gliders and birds to gain height.

throttle Like the accelerator of a car, this device controls the power of an aircraft engine.

thrust The force developed by a propeller or jet engine that drives an airplane through the air.

tiltrotor A tiltrotor uses its rotors to take off or land vertically, like a helicopter, then tilts its rotors to fly forward like a plane.

traffic pattern The rectangular flight pattern for aircraft around a landing runway at an airport.

transonic Flying through the sound barrier.

VFR (Visual Flight Rules) A set of procedures or "rules of the road" for pilots flying in daytime conditions and primarily with the use of visual references.

V/STOL An abbreviation for vertical and/or short takeoff and landing.

wing flap A hinged section of the wing that is lowered when landing and taking off to increase lift at low speed.

wing slat A small airfoil that forms a gap at the front of the wing to increase lift at low speed.

World War I A war involving many of the world's nations, fought between 1914 and 1918.

World War II A war involving many of the world's nations, fought between 1939 and 1945.

yaw The aerodynamic term that describes an airplane's nose swinging from side to side.

Index

Credits

The publisher thanks Robert Coupe for his contribution, and Jo Rudd for the index.

Key tl=top left; tc=top center; tr=top right; cl=center left; c=center; bl=bottom left; br=bottom right

MAPS
Andrew Davies/Creative Communication

ILLUSTRATIONS
Front cover Malcolm Godwin/Moonrunner Design; **Back cover** Godd.com tr; Malcolm Godwin/Moonrunner Design c, bl; **Spine** Malcolm Godwin/Moonrunner Design

Malcolm Godwin/Moonrunner Design 10–11, 12–13, 14–15, 26–7, 28–9, 30–1, 40–1, 44–5, 46–7, 50–1, 54–5, 58–9, 61; **Godd.com (Markus Junker, Rolf Schröter, Patrik Tilp)** 8–9, 16–17, 18–19, 20–1, 22–3, 24–5, 34–5, 36–7, 38–9, 42–3, 48–9, 52–3, 56–7, 60–1

PHOTOGRAPHS
CBT=Corbis; GI=Getty Images; NASA=National Aeronautics and Space Administration; NASM=National Air and Space Museum; NHPA=Natural History Photographic Agency; SH=Shutterstock; SPL=Science Photo Library; TPL=photolibrary.com

14br CBT; **16**br CBT; **19**br NHPA; **20**tr GI; **24**bl CBT; **26**tl SPL; **28**cl NASA; **30**tr NASA; **32**tc GI; **34**tl CBT, bl GI; **36**tl GI; **37**br CBT; **38**tl James Gardner (at the Imperial War Museum, Duxford); **40**tl GI; **41**tr GI; **42**tl CBT; **43**tr CBT; **44**tl NASM; **46**tl GI; **48**tl SH; **50**tc GI, bl GI; **52**tl TPL; **54**bl eurocopter.com; **56**tl SPL, bl GI; **58**bl NASA